What Now, God?
Finding God in Transitions

What Now, God? Finding God in Transitions
Copyright ©2022 by Jeanie Shaw

All rights are reserved. No part of this book may be duplicated, copied, translated, reproduced or stored mechanically, digitally or electronically without specific, written permission of the author and publisher.

Printed in the United States of America.

ISBN: 978-1-953623-82-9.

Unless otherwise indicated, all Scripture references are from the Holy Bible, New International Version, copyright 1973, 1978, 1984, 2011 by the International Bible Society. Used by permission of Zondervan Bible Publishers.

Illumination Publishers titles may be purchased in bulk for classroom instruction, business, fund-raising, or sales promotional use. For information please e-mail paul.ipibooks@me.com

Illumination Publishers is committed to caring wisely for God's creation and uses recycled paper whenever possible.

Jeanie Shaw served in the ministry and with HOPE *worldwide* over her forty-seven years in the full-time ministry. Recently widowed, she retired, sold her house, moved to another state, began her doctoral program, and began a few new business ventures. Her deepest joy comes from helping others fall more deeply in love with God, who longs to carry us through life's joys and sorrows. Desiring to see others thrive, she teaches worldwide and writes. This is her seventeenth book. She finds great joy from her friendships with her adult children and their families, and from her forever friendships scattered across the globe.

Contents

Introduction: God Is in the Transitions
5

Chapter One: Transition and Identity
14

Chapter Two: Mourning Transition
43

Chapter Three: Walking Through Candyland
64

Chapter Four: Preparing for Transition
84

Chapter Five: Raise Your Ebenezer: Marking Transitions
109

Chapter Six: Transitions that Overflow
127

Chapter Seven: Courage for the Next Steps
141

Conclusion
155

Appendix: Who God Says We Are
158

Dedication

To the Fergusons: Gordon, my true brother and friend, whose love, counsel, and encouragement provide me with friendship, guidance, and courage to step forward beyond my comfort zones throughout many transitions. And Theresa, whose constant prayer cover and kindness fill me with strength. You are forever friends and family.

And to my children and their families, who shower with me with never-ending love as we all navigate transitions. I am deeply blessed.

Introduction:
God Is in the Transitions

A few hours ago I trekked down the path to the town center in a snow-covered New England mountain village to watch New Year's Eve fireworks. The noisy, festive, and colorful displays of fire marked the transition from last year to this. Like fireworks, personal transitions bring explosions. Fireworks come in all extremes, varying between earsplitting multicolored beauties and smoke-filled duds. So do personal transitions. As I watched, I heard gasps of awe from those embracing the celebration, along with some cries of fear from several children (and a few dogs) who were frightened by the commotion. In a final goodbye to 2021, the fireworks crescendoed into a grand finale of flashes and blasts, signaling the end of the celebration. An eerie silence followed. *Is that it? What's next? The old is gone, but what can I expect going forward?*

It feels right to begin a book about transitions during this annual celebration of an ending and a beginning. This is the start of my third new year as a widow. The first day of January feels a little lonely ever since my husband died, marking yet another year that holds both emptiness and hope. This past year, transitions rolled through my life like a freight train. I sold my house of thirty-plus years and bought a new one, moved to another state, retired, and began my doctorate program. My oldest granddaughter graduated and my youngest started preschool. The whole world remained in a pandemic, with ever-changing protocols. Transitions happen to everyone, but sometimes they come fast and furious, like the fireworks finale. As I walked back to my cozy winter cabin, remnants of ashes and clutter littered the snow-surrounded site where the fireworks had been launched less than an hour before. When surveying the remnants of our own transitions, we feel the results of the explosions, often seeing only burnt remains no longer resembling anything beautiful. The past has happened. Now what?

Transitions invite us to new seasons of exuberant growth, or they can lead us to disappointment and disillusionment. Once-stable situations turn upside down, along with our emotions. How do we find meaning in these transitions? Where can our disoriented, anger-filled, grief-numbed, confused, fearful, or even excited selves find God?

Life changes can hit us in the gut with such force that we barely recognize who we are after they hit. We ask, "What now, God?" as we search for him amid jolting, faith-challenging transitions, both big and small.

Transitions Happen

We only get to choose some transitions. Some are exciting, others we dread, but all of them produce turmoil. They are often unavoidable and uninvited—but are

Introduction

necessary parts of life. Can you imagine if nothing ever changed? What if the sun didn't rise and set, the tide failed to turn, or the seasons stood still? What if we never grew up? Life without transition would be stagnant. While we know we need transitions, our hearts can feel ill-prepared for their arrival. Change is hard, but ready or not, it will come. Unless we take time to assess our transitions, we can plow through them without realizing their presence or their impact. What kinds of transitions first come to your mind?

- If you go way back, perhaps you remember starting school or changing schools. The process was likely both scary and exciting. You were away from home for a few hours for the first time. I remember running away from kindergarten, all the way home to hide in my garage because I forgot my lunch money and thought I would end up in "school jail." I should have learned from that incident that transitions would bring me angst.
- Maybe your childhood innocence was stolen by abuse or family dysfunction. You transitioned from childhood too abruptly, before your time. Your family may have changed due to divorce, loss, abuse, or addiction.
- Graduation brought transition. Whether you went to college or directly into the work force, transition may have burdened you with questions like: How will I pay for this? Where will I live? What do I want to do

with my life? How do I do laundry?
- Perhaps you experienced a move, or two, or thirty-seven! Moves are big deals, even if we initiate them.
- Your path may have taken a turn resulting from a break-up, divorce, or death in the family.
- Your decision to become a Christian transformed your priorities, values, and some friendships. It's an amazing change, but not an easy transition. Or perhaps you have not changed like you hoped you would after this decision, and you feel defeated.
- Do you remember landing that first job? Then, remember when you first changed jobs by force or by choice? Each change produced a domino reaction of other changes.
- Perhaps you lost a close friendship due to unresolved conflicts or simply because you both took different paths.
- Marriage was a huge transition. And just when you were somewhat accustomed to living with another person 24/7, a small human joined the family. And then came another, and maybe another. Each change brought some crazy transitions.
- Maybe you dreamed of having a family and couldn't have children—your "family" mindset had to change, and it felt crushing.
- Maybe you wished to be married but never found the right person. This requires a huge transition of your

Introduction

dreams, and grief often stays close by.
- More job changes happened. You may have had financial challenges and had to move again. You left friends behind, or they moved away and left you behind.
- Someone you love may have developed a health challenge, or may have died. Life seemed to stop for you, but not for others.
- You may have developed health challenges. Everything changes then. What was simple is now hard, and few understand.
- Your kids leave the nest.
- You lose interest in your job.
- You change your views on what is most important in life.
- You question some of your core values, presuppositions, and beliefs.
- You get disappointed and are tempted to feel disillusioned with job, church, family, or things near and dear to your heart, and you wonder if you will ever gain back your joy and trust.
- Everyone around you seems to be in transition too, and it's hard to think from others' perspectives when your life is in turmoil.
- Retirement brought many changes to your life, and to your spouse's life—you aren't used to being around each other all day and sometimes wish you could go back to the way it was. Married or single, you may

experience a new loneliness, lacking purpose.
- You realize you are getting older...and at times feel like a "has been" and no longer relevant.
- You come face to face with your mortality.

Can you relate? I am convinced that we need to talk more about transitions in our lives, seeking to understand the oft-hidden ways they affect us and to find ways we can grow stronger and closer to God as we adjust to new normals—that don't yet feel so normal.

One of my favorite memories as a child growing up in Florida is of my dad as he taught me to ride the ocean waves. He helped me find the perfect curl of the wave that could carry me to shore. When I caught it just right, I would go so far ashore that my swimsuit filled with sand and my knees scraped across the beach. What a glorious sensation to feel the current's power carrying me along. Resisting only ruined the experience; I just had to let go and ride it in. If I close my eyes, I can still feel the immense force of the waves rolling around me, sweeping through from my feet to my outstretched arms. It felt exhilarating. The bigger the wave, the scarier yet more wonderful it was. If I missed the curl, the waves would either crash on me or pass me by. I learned to duck under the ones that were cresting before I was ready. I like to think that finding God during transitions is like finding that curl of the wave. As with jumping into a wave, it's not always easy to "jump into God," but I believe this is the only spiritually formative way to navigate transitions. It

Introduction

is only possible because God has been willing to "jump into us." Let that sink in. God in me. God's power is so much bigger than we have yet tasted or experienced. It can sweep us up and carry us through waves of change that take us to places yet unknown. His power gives us all we need, and he provides it freely. He became human so that we could experience divinity and ride this divine power through every transition in life.

> *His divine power has given us everything we need for a godly life through our knowledge of him who called us by his own glory and goodness.*
>
> *Through these he has given us his very great and precious promises, so that through them you may participate in the divine nature, having escaped the corruption in the world caused by evil desires.* (2 Peter 1:3–4)

Sometimes, even if an approaching wave is small, we remember a time when a big one took our breath away and sent us swirling out of control, leaving us fearful that we would drown. We forget that God is stronger than the waves and longs to carry us through them. Fear is often rooted in memories of previous, painful transitions. When we better understand our hesitancies, we can gain confidence to try again, holding to God's promises while riding in the curl of the wave. If we lose sight of him, a spinning spiral of waves crashes over us before we can even stand up again! Thankfully, God knows the emotions that come with transitions, because in Jesus, he experienced them. This helps me. A lot. He can navigate you into the curl of the wave and ride with you to the shore. So, if God can carry us through our constant transitions, why do they keep rocking us and pulling us under?

At the core of spiritually transforming transitions lies the need to understand who God is and who we are. In the following chapters we will explore ways men and women in the Bible navigated change and then consider our own contexts. We will explore the importance of our identity. We will learn to lament, spend time in the desert, practice commemoration, and listen for God's call, allowing him to find us. At the end of each chapter, I have included questions for further reflection and life stories from faithful men and women who describe ways they find God amid transitions. They have found, albeit with struggle, the curl of the wave. They share what it means to them to be taken by the hand and guided by the Holy Spirit through their transitions.

> *But when the Friend comes, the Spirit of the Truth, he will take you by the hand and guide you into all the truth there is. He won't draw attention to himself, but will make sense out of what is about to happen and, indeed, out of all that I have done and said.* (John 16:13 MSG)

Introductory Reflections

Reflect on transitions that have felt most significant for you. What transition(s) brought you:

Joy? _____

Fear? _____

Sadness? _____

Shame? _____

Relief? _____

Anger? _____

Confusion? _____

Choose several transitions and identify your emotions that accompany them. What does this reflection tell you about the significance of these transitions?

Chapter 1: Transition and Identity

"What do you do?" This oft-asked question can tempt us to place our value in our function in life rather than in relational, heart-centered qualities that reflect our true value. Few other questions bring to our minds quick judgments, pride, shame, or even "imposter syndrome."[1] How do we change this tendency? How can we view ourselves through the lens of love rather than function? We begin by exploring experiences that have shaped our concept of identity and compare them to God's viewpoint. We often see ourselves through distorted lenses because we live in a fallen world that has difficulty accepting God's perspective. The varied ways we perceive our identities have far-reaching effects, including ways we process transitions.

In 1998, we adopted a twelve-year-old Romanian boy who had spent all his childhood years in a cinderblock orphanage. He knew no English, never experienced family, and had gone through two grades of school. Through parenting him, I became more closely acquainted with the role identity plays in transitions. As would be expected, his struggle for identity runs deep—loss, shame, rejection, difficulty to trust, and desire for control remain

---

[1]. Imposter syndrome is when a person has difficulty believing that their successes or accomplishments are legitimately achieved through their own efforts or talents.

close, constant companions. His view of his worth—someone loveable, valuable, and created in the image of God—often eludes him. If he could only realize his true identity as one loved by God rather than shaped by shame and rejection, I believe it would alter his entire perspective. He is not alone, however. We all have identity crises. We may not have grown up in a similar environment, but we all carry marred identities. No matter our background, transitions challenge our sense of identity.

Even though I grew up in a loving family, I have struggled at various times in my life with people-pleasing in order to feel accepted, thinking I must prove myself to show my worth. At other times I have held perfectionist standards, to feel more acceptable to God and others. Such deep-rooted tendencies in our lives often stem from unresolved convictions about our true identities, and our acceptance of who God says we are—his beloved. This identity crisis has appeared since the beginning of humankind, passing through generations of misguided perspectives and practices. We can learn of identity struggles from numerous men and women in the Bible. Moses and Naomi are two such individuals whose life transitions show us the importance of discovering the identity God intends for us.

Moses' Search for Identity

The LORD replied, "My Presence will go with you, and I will give you rest." Then Moses said to him, "If your Presence does not go with us, do not send us up from here.

How will anyone know that you are pleased with me and with your people unless you go with us? What else will distinguish me and your people from all the other people on the face of the earth?" (Exodus 33:14–16)

In these words from Exodus 33, we discover perhaps the most crucial factor in transitioning well—the link between our identity and God's presence.

Moses experienced challenging transitions as he was born an Israelite but adopted into Egyptian royalty. He was called to lead his birth nation from slavery in Egypt, passing through the wilderness to the promised land. Throughout his life he experienced separation from his family and country, adoption, moves, royalty, more moves, floods, famine, betrayal, and isolation. His confused identity got the best of him through his anger when he killed an Egyptian who had mistreated one of "his own people." Later, Moses' future wife, Zipporah, introduced him to her father as an Egyptian although he was born a Jew. Exodus 2:22 tells us that Moses named his son Gershom because, he said, "I have become a foreigner in a foreign land." We can easily miss the significance of Moses' identity struggle. If anger got the best of Moses, a man considered the humblest man on the face of the earth (Numbers 12:3), we shouldn't be surprised when negative emotions accompany our identity struggles.

God graciously allowed Moses needed time in solitude in the town of Midian after his anger got the best of him. Here in the wilderness, he would come to terms with who he was and who he was meant to be. "Desert time" becomes a common theme in the Bible for recalibrating one's identity. There seems no shortcut to times in the wilderness or in the desert. Moses needed a heart transformation to fulfill his calling to lead the Israelites out of slavery. He experienced God's presence. His time in the desert helped him come to terms with his identity and find a deep relationship with God. Author Ruth Haley Barton describes this transformation:

> So after weeks and months in solitude, the chaos in Moses' soul settled a bit. He began to make sense of his own history, and he was finally able to say, "This is who I am. The experience of living as an alien in a foreign land is what has shaped me." Finally, he had come home to himself. All of us have need for this kind of homecoming in which we claim our experiences as our own and acknowledge the ways they have shaped us. Then we are in a position to take responsibility for ourselves rather than being driven by our unconscious patterns of manipulating and controlling reality.[2]

We must all determine whether we have come home to ourselves before we can successfully take responsibility for ourselves. If we haven't "come home," we will be tempted to avoid or manipulate reality. But

---

2. Ruth Haley Barton, *Strengthening the Soul of Your Leadership* (Downer Groves, IL: IVP, 2008), 48.

how do we find our way home? Reframing our identity takes intentional time and contemplation, something we often avoid. If we try to accomplish life and its transitions without understanding our identity, then anger, shame, confusion, and disillusionment will eventually get the best of us. Moses needed to sort this out, and I dare say we all have sorting to do. Let's not shortcut the time we need to understand who and whose we are. It takes time to quiet and empty ourselves enough to allow God's loving presence to reshape our identity. When we really believe that God's presence is with us, our identity more closely aligns with him. He is with us. We are with him. He is around us, surrounding us, and most importantly in us. God's presence living within us changes everything about our identity. We bear his image. His presence must wrap its way around our hearts and minds, enveloping our souls in such a way that when we are asked "what do you do?" we realize that this question has little connection with our identity. We can feel confident and assured that God's presence with and within us changes everything.

Naomi: Our View of God Determines Our Self-View

Naomi is another person in the Bible whose misplaced identity kept her, at first, from finding peace in transition. After losing her husband and her two sons, she began a journey back to her homeland. She misplaced her God-given identity, so much so that she changed her name from Naomi (meaning pleasant) to Mara, or "bitter." She felt unloved by God, as if he were against her (Ruth 1:20-21). Her identity had changed because her view of God had changed. Only when she saw herself as God saw her could she once again find new purpose and meaning for her broken life (Ruth 4:14–17).

Alicia Britt Chole, in her excellent book *40 Days of Decrease* writes, "For the faithful Christ-follower, self-concept is inextricably connected to God-concept. We are valuable because God is creator. We are forgiven because God is redeemer. If God is not who we thought he was, then who are we?"[3] Our self-identity grows out of our view of God, not from what we do. Naomi rediscovered God's care for her, and no longer felt bitter. She remembered who he was. The forces of evil always seek to distort our views of God and ourselves, accusing us in all kinds of ways, including labeling us with false identities (Revelation 12:10).

Identity Is Not Defined by Function

Satan, the accuser, tried to skew Jesus' identity as God in the flesh. Jesus was tempted by Satan to use the power of the Spirit to *do* something to prove that he was the Son of God. Perhaps this temptation was for Jesus to find his role affirmation, his self-identity, his value, his meaning, and his purpose through a functional approach.[4] While we don't know for sure, we know he was tempted in all ways like we are (Hebrews 4:15).

---

3. Alicia Britt Chole, *40 Days of Decrease* (Nashville, TN: Thomas Nelson, 2016), 21.

4. Robert Mulholland, *Shaped by the Word: The Power of Scripture in Spiritual Formation* (Nashville, TN: Upper Room, 2001), 90.

What Now, God?

Thankfully, he never forgot where he had come from and where he was going (John 13:3). He knew who he was, and this made all the difference throughout the transitions and temptations he faced.

The world calls us to perceive our identity as something to be controlled and manipulated for personal purposes, insisting that we can determine our own self-image by how effectively we grasp or do certain things. In our world of selfies, humanity screams to be seen, to be recognized, and to be loved. The world values beauty, wealth, brains, athleticism, and success. But this does not define anyone. None of these things last. *What you do* does not define you. *What you have* does not define you. Whether young or old, we are defined by our worth before God, not our function or accomplishments. Misplaced sources of identity can have life and death consequences. Sharing his thoughts on identity, author Robert Mulholland notes:

> They [our youth] are being raised in a culture that tends to postpone meaningful functional activity until the early or mid-twenties (the cutoff line for the peak in the teen suicide rate!). Thus our youth are caught in a tremendously ambiguous situation; their value, meaning, identity, and purpose depend on their functional role in society, but they are not allowed to have a significant functional role. Is it any wonder that suicide, drug abuse, and crime all have peak representations in this age group?[5]

---

5. Mulholland, 86.

He continues to explain that a similar phenomenon connecting identity with function happens with the retired. Statistics show that the suicide rate among senior citizens is twice that of the teenage group. "One morning they wake up and the functional role which, for a lifetime, has given their life meaning, value, purpose, and identity is no longer there. The functional support structure for their sense of self-image and self-esteem is gone."[6]

When we assess our identity, meaning, value, and purpose through function, over time we are left with disillusionment, dissatisfaction, and disappointment. Our relevancy comes from our identity in Christ. Everything else doesn't last.

Christlike Transition to Irrelevancy

Theologian, professor, and priest Henri Nouwen allowed his transitions to give his life a paradigm shift from function to identity through Christ. His perspective challenges my heart as he shares his entrance into the world of the L'Arche community, working with the mentally handicapped. He describes his transition from a relevant, active, respected, educated leader to a new paradigm where he was faced with his "naked self, open for affirmations and rejections, hugs and punches, smiles and tears all dependent simply on how I was perceived at the moment [through the eyes of the mentally handicapped man he was serving.]"[7]

---

6. Mulholland, 86.
7. Henri J. Nouwen, *In the Name of Jesus*, (New York: Crossroad, 1989), 28.

What Now, God?

Nouwen reminds us that Jesus did not come to prove himself but to empty himself. He proposes a question. Do we seek to prove ourselves or empty ourselves? If our transitions leave us feeling we have something we must prove, we still have work to do in accepting our God-given identity.

Nouwen's life transition from Harvard professor and priest to volunteer caretaker for a man with extreme mental handicaps moved his view of himself to greater irrelevancy. He explains, "The leaders of the future will be those who dare to claim their irrelevance in the contemporary world as a divine vocation that allows them to enter into a deep solidarity with the anguish underlying all the glitter of success and to bring the light of Jesus there."[8] Nouwen suggests that when we truly understand and accept Jesus' love for us, we discard our personal relevance in exchange for giving ourselves away to others. Understanding our identity allows us to become givers from the outflow of our hearts, even when our identities get tested throughout various stages of life transitions.

While we are free to make choices of what we will and will not do, the choices should be made *because of* who we are, not to *determine* who we are. It is out of this understanding of our own identity that we can give to others out of the fullness of God in us. John Kronstadt, a nineteenth-century monk, illustrates this truth. In recounting his story, author James Bryan Smith shares:

---

8. Nouwen, *In the Name*, 35.

> Alcohol abuse around him was rampant but the other priests would wait for the hurting to come to them rather than go out to them. John, compelled by love, would lift the hungover and foul-smelling from the gutter and cradle them in his arms as he told them, "This is beneath your dignity. You were meant to house the fullness of God." That describes you and me. Knowing this is our true identity is the secret to walking in holiness.[9]

This is also the secret to successful, God-glorifying, and peace-filled transitions. I have had to wrestle with making choices because of who I am rather than to determine who I am. I don't think I am alone.

Who Am I Now?

For forty-five years I was Wyndham's wife. For most of those years I was employed in full-time ministry. I was a familiar friend and neighbor on Patriot Road, where I had lived for over three decades. I'm now a widow and retired, living in another state. I'm no one's wife and have no recognized occupation. My neighbors are still strangers, though I'm trying to change that as I meet more of them.

I miss my husband, who bore witness to my life and whose life I witnessed. He worried for my safety when I hiked, always making sure I took the dog with me. He knew the things that brought me joy and that would hurt

---

9. James Bryan Smith, *The Good and Beautiful God* (Westmont, IL: IVP, 2009), 162.

me. He drew out my emotions and wiped away tears. He always wanted my opinion for his thoughts. My parents, who have been gone for decades, also cared about the details of my life. Who else but my mom searched what my weather forecast would be each day or had the uncanny ability to make a birthday card arrive on the exact date of my birthday? My children and grandchildren are my greatest treasures, but they cannot define me.

I had to learn to accept that God cares for *me,* but it is harder to believe because I have never physically seen God like I have seen my family. No wonder Jesus tells the gang, after reassuring Thomas' doubt of his resurrection, "Blessed are those who have not seen and yet have believed" (John 20:29). The core of my identity rests in whether I believe and accept that Jesus loves me. This must be enough.

I no longer gain identity as someone's wife, my parents' daughter, or as a full-time minister. Though my husband treated me with profound respect, a woman's voice is still evolving in the church. When Wyndham's illness forced his early retirement, soon afterward I was asked to change my role in the ministry. It came as a shock and hit me like a ton of bricks. It was a transition I did not expect or want.

My job, leading (I much prefer the term "serving") women's ministry in the church, was my one sense of normalcy in my otherwise chaotic world where my husband lay on a hospital bed dying at home. My best friends were my colleagues, and the job was going well for those I served and for me. When this happened, I felt like I had been kicked in the gut and run over. It was a difficult transition for many reasons. I cried to God with loud cries and tears, crying myself to sleep for days. Everything felt taken from me. With my husband dying and my job changing, I felt placed in a desert with paralyzing grief. While I still prefer that this change had not happened, it was in the pain and solitude where I came to grips with my identity and gained new confidence. My sense of normalcy could not be my husband's health or my job. I held fiercely to Jesus and felt his presence in indescribable ways. He understood. He has been misunderstood, he has felt everything I have ever felt in infinite proportions, yet was able to fully love in return. He experienced loss, rejection, and separation from his eternal home, and was acquainted with grief. He knew where he had come from and where he was going (John 13:3). I need this identity assurance ringing continually in my ears and in my heart. On my best days, I too know where I come from and where I am going. Because of Jesus' certitude of his identity, he is a secure place for me to land. I can count on God who is, was, and always will be. I can count on his love, and through him I gain my identity.

This is the God I can run to. This is the one who will hold me close. This is the one who will show himself to me, but only if I still myself enough to listen, watch, and "know that [he is] God" (Psalm 46:10). He is the one who wants to know my thoughts and cares about my weather forecast. He even *makes* my weather! He shows himself to me in ways I can miss if I don't slow down and look for him. Be still. Be still and know. Be still and know he is God.

God Reveals Himself

Though I love to study the Bible, exegete, and learn cultural and archaeological backgrounds of Scripture, two things have taught me the most about God's love for me this past year. Simple things. The first was after a morning of tears, wishing I could know more about paradise and Wyndham's state of being. *Can he see me? How much awareness is there? Does he know I moved?* I know he is with God; I just don't know what that looks like. As I was cry-praying ugly tears, I asked God to calm my heart and to somehow let me know he was okay... that it was all okay. Those were my words. I got up and my phone rang. A sister, whom I didn't know well and seldom talked to, called with one message. She said she didn't know why but felt urged to call me to "let me know everything is okay." Those were her words. She did not understand why she had this strong urge and thought I would think her call was very weird. It was certainly not weird. It was a reminder that God does indeed "care about my weather." I am known to him, and my identity is in him. His presence with me is the distinguishing factor of my life.

The second display of God's tender love reassured me that he was continually transforming me. A few months ago, immediately following my move to Connecticut, I began walking along the Connecticut River every day. I feel a serene closeness to God as I walk and as I watch the river's ever-changing movement. Right after my transition to Connecticut, a lone goose moved into the dock at the river across the street. This goose remained there and would walk right up to me. This felt significant to me because years ago, I studied the patterns of geese when a lone goose "adopted" my parents after losing its mate. My parents had a pond in their backyard, and instead of swimming in the pond, the goose stayed by my parents, standing outside the glass window on the back porch. He followed them everywhere. After my dad died, the mail carrier often had trouble entering the yard because the goose tried to protect my mother.

When a goose loses its mate (they mate for life) they are suddenly alone, and they can "imprint," or adopt a nearby person as their new mate. I thought this lone goose that I passed each day was a special little hug from God during my huge transition and move following widowhood and retirement. For three months the goose was there, and then suddenly it was gone. I felt that this gift from God (and perhaps Wyndham, who knows?) was there for as long as I needed it. Each day I thanked God for this meaningful gift, but I missed the goose after it was gone. One day soon after, while at the river, I asked God if perhaps he was telling me that he thought I had enough time for adjustment and that it was now time for me to fly. I boldly asked him, if it wasn't too crazy a request, to now put an eagle in my path. That same day as I was walking, I spotted a bald eagle across the river. I had not seen it before. Then, something spectacular happened. The eagle took flight and flew across the river directly over my head. Honestly, it was all I could do not to fall down on the ground and praise God for such kindness. I cried in gratitude, and I cry again as I type this remembrance. I know it is time to fly. After the phone call of "everything is okay," this was the second hug I received this year. God stays close to me in transitions. Yes, God speaks to us through his word, but God and the Bible are not the same thing. He does not quit revealing himself. He is still alive, dynamic, and living in us, his image bearers. We can "jump into him," because he has "jumped into us."

Healthy Transitions Begin with Healthy Identities

Healthy, spiritually-forming transitions begin with a long, hard look at the ways we view and assign our identity. If we view ourselves by our function, upbringing, relationships, accomplishments, or life stages we will stumble. The waves will crash down on our heads. We can try to avoid them, but before we gather our balance from one wave, another will soon come crashing down, knocking us over. We must learn to find the sweet spot in the curl of the wave, in the shadow of his wings, in the cleft of the rock, and carried close to his heart.

It takes decisive work to accept our identities as God's beloved. If we don't do the hard work necessary to wrestle away our long-held functional (or dysfunctional) identity and exchange it for our God-given identity, we will continually default to our old views when change comes. It happened when Moses reacted with anger before he spent time in Midian and it happened with "Maura" before she reclaimed her identity with God on her journey home. God was working behind the scenes to involve her in his grand redemption story in Jesus, through the lineage of the daughter-in-law she loved and cared for. We may forget who we are, but thankfully God always knows who he is and works on our behalf, even when we cannot see it. Naomi never saw Jesus' birth, the plan of our redemption. Moses never entered the promised land, but he heard God and walked with him. God works on our behalf because he knows who and whose we are.

A parable about Michelangelo forming a statue goes like this:

> There was once a sculptor who worked hard with hammer and chisel on a large block of marble. A little child who was watching him saw nothing more than large and small pieces of stone falling away left and right. He had no idea what was happening. But when the boy returned to the studio a few weeks later, he saw, to his surprise, a large, powerful lion sitting in the place where the marble had stood. With great excitement, the boy ran to the sculptor and said, "Sir, tell me, how did you know there was a lion in the marble?" The sculptor answered, "I knew there was

a lion in the marble because before I saw a lion in the marble, I saw him in my own heart."[10]

Thank God that as our sculptor, he can carve away the protective armor from which we try to find our value, meaning, and identity. We are made in God's image. Never forget that. And to understand this image, we must never forget who God is.

When we forget who God is and thus misinform our identity as his image bearers, destructive patterns are sure to follow. We will try to prove ourselves worthy and loveable. We will get down on ourselves, will lose vision for our lives, become jealous, or become apathetic. We will then search for ways to fill this void through function or by numbing our feelings through destructive habits. The best approach is to soak in our true identity. The way we live springs from the identity we hold to. In the appendix, I have included a list of scriptures stating who God says we are. I recommend reading them often. Read them out loud until you believe them.

Godspeed

We must make adequate time to find and accept our God-given identity. I like to hurry and take shortcuts but was reminded, through reading a book called *Three Mile an Hour God*,[11] that Jesus spent a great deal of time walk-

---

10. Henri Nouwen, *Spiritual Direction: Wisdom for the Long Walk of Faith* (NY: Harper One, 2018), 16–17.
11. Kosuke Koyama, *Three Mile an Hour God* (London: SCM Press, 2021).

ing, usually with others. The speed of walking is about three miles an hour. Therefore, the author opines, since Jesus is God incarnate, God has a speed. God is love; thus love has a speed that cannot be found when we try to outpace him. Our transitions require reflection, which can become uncomfortable, but we must not shortcut this step. Often, we will need some guidance and counsel from friends or even professionals to "go there," especially if we have experienced trauma. It takes hard work to discover ways our identities have been formed, misinformed, and deformed through the years. Discovery gets unpleasant and painful, but realizing and naming the pain becomes freeing. We must learn that it is enough to be made in his image and to be loved by him. When we believe this, we can live in peace and more brilliantly reflect that image. If our identity depends on anything else, we are sure to stumble.

At this point, you may be thinking. *Nice idea. I would love time to explore my identity. I would love to walk three miles an hour through life, hand in hand with God. Maybe on some other planet that would work for me. But may I introduce you to my family responsibilities, work demands, financial challenges, caregiving responsibilities, physical and mental health challenges...not to mention church responsibilities?*

I hear you. Take heart. Times change, and as the wisdom literature teaches us, there is a season for everything (Ecclesiastes 3:1–8). In my current stage of life, I have more available time for reflection than ever before. While some of our life situations cannot currently change, we can often make choices in more areas than we realize. They may be hard choices, such as job opportunities that pay less but allow us to live life outside of work, less time on devices, and fewer extracurricular activities. All choices should be vetted by God, others we trust, and with our core values in mind. Too often, our busyness comes from our desire to prove our value, worth, or acceptance. We must search our heart and values, but I believe if we are too busy to find the time to just be with God, we are too busy. Try a social media, television, or sports fast for a week. You may be surprised at how much time you find. If you have young children, remember the transitions will happen fast. There are many things that I could have added to life years ago, and though sometimes I may have added too much, I knew I could never get those years back. I did what I could. That is all you can do, but it would serve you well to check the reasons you do what you do. You may find the reasons stem from your views of yourself and of God.

Once we learn and accept the identity assigned to us as his beloved, we can then stretch out our arms and feel a power like none other "in the curl of God" carrying us to shore. Maybe we will arrive with sand in our swimsuit and scraped legs, but it is a glorious thing to be carried along by the Holy Spirit, with a power outside ourselves. It feels both frightening and exhilarating.

Our stories of Identity in Transitions

Unhappy Birthday?
By Hannah DeSouza
Chișinău, Moldova

Looking back ten years ago, October 7, 2011–Beal High School, UK:

Whether we spoke it aloud or not, many of us would confess that from a young age we started to form a timeline in our heads. While each person's may vary a little, the usual culprits are typically: a time by which we expected to have our career on track; to have found 'the one'; to get married; to own a home; to have a baby; to have two babies; to get that qualification, or to have accomplished [insert goal here].

Family, media, culture, even church culture, can perpetuate some of these elusive milestones we're meant to have reached by a certain point. Yet for many of us—dare I say, most of us—these timelines rarely align with reality. Birthdays, in this light, can be an annual cold-water-to-the-face reminder that *we are not where we thought we would be at this point in our lives.*

Such is true for me as I type this on my twenty-eighth birthday from my room in Chișinău, Moldova. Far (2000-miles-away far) from the timeline this rosy-cheeked girl had in her head and heart when she blew out her eighteenth birthday candles in the sixth-form common room. I almost feel like I owe that girl an explanation or should at least warn her. The words of the shrunken head from the Knight Bus in *Harry Potter* come to mind: "It's goin' ta be a bumpy ride!"

I hope the following words I've decided to share with her instead will be more beneficial.

What Now, God?

There's a lot to come in this next decade of life, so let me prepare you:

You are going to cry a lot; you'll laugh a lot too.

You'll figure out the genres of music that stir your heart and the movies that make you sob.

You'll discover a passion for literature as you find kindred spirits through pages, despite living centuries apart (human nature really doesn't change that much).

You'll learn that you're an ENFP[12] that needs both people and solitude.

In a few years, you will discover the Enneagram of Personality (thanks Ryane). Don't listen to the people who say it puts you in a box! For you it will feel like the lid is being taken off a box you were already in, only now the contents are illuminated.

You will come to realize that knowing yourself—what refreshes you, what your gifts are, and what makes you come alive—is not a selfish endeavor; rather, it is one of the greatest gifts you can give to people and your community.

A key lesson you will learn is that you will not be able to please everyone, nor were you meant to (Galatians 1:10).

---

12. An ENFP is someone with the Extraverted, Intuitive, Feeling, and Prospecting personality traits.16–17.

You will grasp the importance of finding safe places and people for your doubts and will discover that questioning and wrestling is good when it leads to hard-won convictions (they're much stronger than inherited ones, trust me).

You will better understand that the church is a divine concept: dreamed up in heaven, but lived out on a fallen earth. In this you will learn to be patient with yourself and fellow believers as we try to realize the vision together.

You will push through your anxiety of public speaking and performing and in them discover that joy is often waiting just around the corner of your fears.

Although you are scared to navigate the London Underground alone, you will soon find yourself traveling the world, making lifelong friends along the way.

Some friendships will feel handcrafted for a particular season, while others will stretch through several, even becoming permanent fixtures—both are gifts.

You will live abroad and learn how to drive on the left *and* righthand sides of the road (with no accidents so far, just some close calls...).

Don't feel guilty when you find out you prefer coffee to tea (from when I last checked, you can still keep your British citizenship).

What Now, God?

Through traveling, your concept of home is going to change; you will find it wrapped up in people more than places. And, of course, wherever Bella is (yes, mum and dad will actually cave in and get a dog).

Over the coming years you will see the doors to some of your dreams open wide, while others remain closed or even shut in your face—don't be disheartened. Through them you will discover that disappointment is a better teacher and character builder than success ever was.

Through sadness you will come to the realization that it is better to be sorrowful if it drives you to God than to be content and far from him. So steward your sorrows well because, despite how they feel, they won't be permanent guests.

In a few short years you will become an auntie (!) and you will find that your heart is able to expand to contain more than you thought it could.

You will love and be loved in return; sometimes it will hurt, other times it will heal, but love will always be worth pursuing.

It will be a rare occurrence, but at times you will get angry—study it. Buried in the anger will be the causes you feel passionate about.

Transition and Identity

Did I mention you'll cry a lot? And laugh a lot?

And just when you think you're standing on a strong foundation you can build a life on, it's going to fall right through. But don't panic! Only then will you discover the strength of the hands that are waiting to catch you on the other side.

Hands that were, in fact, always there.

At twenty-eight you'll have just begun to learn not to get your security or value from external things, and it will be a painful, heart-achingly beautiful lesson. Oh, and you'll also be celebrating this birthday on the mission field in Eastern Europe at the tail end of a global pandemic (surprise!).

Ten years later, my birthday, October 7, 2021–Chisinau, Moldova. With fellow Kingdom dreamers:

Before my eighteen-year-old self panics, I will end with the reminder that this was the Son of God's resumé, age approximately thirty-three:

- Spouse/Children: None
- Qualifications: None
- Home: None
- Social Media Following: Zero
- Popularity: Tentative
- Friends: Few
- Assets: Few
- Purpose: Certain
- Value: Priceless

What Now, God?

With none of the traditional things that give a person value and security, Jesus lived a life of purpose and complete fullness. I hope living with that knowledge can help you walk with your head a little higher today. Knowing that, with the Shepherd at your side, there is nothing you lack—wherever you may be, or may not be, on your timeline. So let's throw the timeline out altogether, shall we?

The LORD is my shepherd;
I have all that I need. (Psalm 23:1 NLT)

The Two Angelas
By Angela Christoffel
Westford, Massachusetts

(This is an excerpt taken from *The Sacred Journey: Finding God in Caregiving,* edited by Jeanie Shaw)

If you knew me in the late '90s, you would see a woman who loved God, was overconfident in her abilities, ran marathons, wore power suits, and wanted to cure the world of injustice. I believed in the power of my education and talents, sometimes more than I believed in God. I was a lawyer fighting for the indigent population, taking on housing issues, domestic violence cases, and employment issues. Fast forward to the present day—you see a woman who is desperate for God's help and grace, runs to and from her daughter's doctors' appointments, wears leggings and a hoodie (most likely stained in a few places), and wants to care for her special-needs daughter with extremely difficult chronic medical conditions and the rest of her family in the best way possible. This is the tale of two Angelas, the first considered successful by the outside world but with a shallow understanding of God and compassion. The second Angela may be viewed by the outside world with pity, and some may even think she is wasting her law degree by being a caregiver. However they do not see the incredible gift that constant caregiving has been to my spiritual walk and my immediate family's life, and the compassion and empathy one can only develop by walking a thin line between the life and death of a young person.

We Are More Than Meets the Eye

Looks are deceptive. God knows there is more to you than your appearance. When I first had Alexa, I was woefully behind in the knowledge of how to parent her and help her navigate her world filled with cognitive disability and chronic, complex medical conditions. She had numerous difficulties as an infant. When she turned one, she had a febrile seizure and the Pandora's Box of the medical intervention world opened before our eyes. From that seizure and further testing, we learned she had an unknown mass growing in her brain. It was decided she would have a needle brain biopsy. That decision would change the rest of our lives. God would use it to refine us as a family and as Christians. After three brain surgeries Alexa's tumor was diagnosed as a low-grade glioma. The tumor caused horrible seizures and cognitive deficits. She endured two different courses of chemotherapy. The last course ended in a long hospitalization for influenza and pneumonia. When she got better and struggled to breathe, we learned she had interstitial lung disease and would need supplemental oxygen. Each year seems to bring a new medical issue that hits us seemingly out of nowhere. Alexa is followed by ten different specialists at Children's Hospital and Dana Farber Institute. Life is in constant transition.

I was a proud woman who made a good living as a lawyer. Much of my self-worth and identity in life and in Christ came from that position. When I was laid off so I could care for Alexa in rehab, I was devastated; however, God knew my heart. He knew I wanted to tenderly love my child and give her all the opportunities I could find to help her to thrive. God knew that I would not be able to do those things while working a demanding full-time job. God guided me to a position as a caretaker, even though it was not my choice. I am humbled, and I need him to make it through each day. I now see my new position as a blessing, but it was hard to appreciate at the time.

God Prepared Me

God allowed me significant training that would help me navigate the medical community's educational issues and the social isolation that accompanies caring for my daughter. Just as God used David's training as a shepherd to slay the giant, he used my training as an attorney to be a caregiver who could conquer the giants of complex medical issues and special needs. My law school loans still haunt us to this day, but without my training as an attorney I would have not known how to fight this battle. I knew how to advocate for my daughter because I had practice advocating for clients. I used my ability to cross-examine witnesses to cross-examine doctors to find the best care protocols and resources.

As David is seen doing many times in the Psalms, I pour my heart out to God. I wish I could say that miraculously Alexa was cured, but that is not the case. Over time though, my heart has found peace in speaking, wailing, crying, and making inaudible utterances to God. This peace, for the most part, stays even when I do not get the answers I want. In turn, God has helped me become a more kind, compassionate, and empathetic person. Do not be afraid to embrace what you feel; God can help you reconcile those feelings and handle them in a godly way.

I am a human, so I mess things up left and right. I can lose my temper when the NutriBullet explodes Alexa's tube-feeding puree all over the ceiling. I fail to show my husband patience, more often than I care to admit. As Alexa likes to say, "True fact, Mom. You can be a hot mess." So if you are a hot mess, do not think that makes you a failure; it makes you human. It makes you like David, who also made mistakes. It is important though, that you take your sins back to God and humbly confess them.

I am not the same Angela I once was, because I have embraced the identity God gave me. The huge life transitions I continually experience allow me to find the curl of the wave as God's power carries me along.

Reflections on Identity

- Reflect on ways you have measured/evaluated/defined your identity through function (what you do). How does this assessment affect you when transitions happen? Reflect on a transition that brings back memories of years-old false messages concerning your identity and consider how you might reframe your assessment.

- Consider how your views of God have affected your views of yourself. Journal your findings.

- In what ways can you relate to Moses, Naomi, or both? What underlying, unresolved emotions might be lingering that become triggered by transitions?

- Moses and Naomi had times of effective solitude to reflect. Prayerfully consider ways you view yourself compared with how God views you. Ask the Spirit to help you believe that you are God's beloved. If you have a lot of deep feelings, perhaps you would benefit from intentional exploratory conversations with a trusted friend and/or professional counseling.

- What does it mean to you to make choices *because* of who you are, not to *determine* who you are?

- Using some of the scriptures in the appendix, write a letter you envision God might write to you concerning who he says you are.

Chapter 2: Mourning Transition

I want to skip this chapter. As a glass-half-full person, a perpetual finder of all the ways something can be done, and ways all can live happily ever after, I don't like to mourn. Honestly, I won't watch a movie until I know that the ending is happy. If a book gets scary or sad, I am "that person" who goes to the last chapter to decide whether I will continue reading. But I have learned to spend time in this lament chapter of life, and I needed time here. I prayed fervently, when my husband was sick, that God would be glorified through his healing. After all, he was needed by so many. We faithfully sought prayers and anointing from fellow elders, just like the Bible says. But the healing didn't happen. His disease got progressively and horrifically worse, and then he died. I learned to mourn.

Jesus evidently thought it important to mourn, since he said, "Blessed are those who mourn, for they will be comforted" (Matthew 5:4). God gave us an entire book of laments in Lamentations. Many psalms describe lament, or mourning. There is something about the mourning process that brings healing and comfort. If we skip over it too quickly, our emotions will overtake us in unexpected ways at unexpected times.

All transitions are hard and need to be mourned and

acknowledged. Even happy transitions bring changes that deserve acknowledgment. Unlamented or unacknowledged grief can surprise us with feelings of anger, depression, or numbness. We may not realize what is hitting us and why. We wonder why we feel snappish or sad; we may simply need to grieve. During these times it is important to do as Jesus did—become "acquainted with grief" (Isaiah 53:3 KJV).

Think of some common transitions and what they bring with them:

- A move often means we can no longer rely on physical visits with close friends like we once enjoyed, or view the scenery and landmarks to which we were accustomed. After my most recent move, my first trip to the grocery store brought great sadness. I didn't know where anything was and saw no familiar faces. I called my daughter and told her I hated my new grocery store. Since then, I found another, and it is okay now. I actually enjoy my new store.

- Personal projects or dreams may run into closed doors, tempting us with discouragement. A job change, even one we desire, leaves behind coworkers and familiarity.

- Families grow up, families mess up, and families split up. These changes become extremely disorienting, and sometimes we don't even know how to do holidays or seat people at special events.

- Health challenges can make most everything we once enjoyed impossible to do—going places, traveling, visiting with friends, enjoying sports, and much more.

- Taking on the caregiving role for a loved one changes everything about your life and schedule. It brings physical strain, anguish, and a lifestyle that has no time for much beyond caregiving. While it is an honor to care for a loved one, the transition brings a sense of not only being swallowed, but if there is no hope for improvement, the anticipatory grief hits hard. The transition to no longer being a caregiver is also difficult, as the world opens its doors again but brings guilt to walk through them when the loved one can't.

- Our last two years in a global pandemic brought unprecedented transitions to life as we knew it. Illness, death, division, isolation, inability to gather with extended family, inability to be with loved ones in hospitals, children in remote learning situations, frazzled health care workers, mental health declines, and isolation fatigue became the norm. We are trying to learn how to deal with the aftermath. We have experienced a global pandemic, but have yet to mourn the transitions.

- Job changes might be good, or they may mean we no longer have a job that seemed a "perfect fit." I mourned my job change. As mentioned earlier, it was not one I desired, and because it was a connection to

normalcy and my closest companions, the loss I felt was intense.
- Job losses or financial setbacks can mean we no longer enjoy a dinner out; instead, we wonder how to keep food on the table. One friend of mine had a period of homelessness. Through his mourning, he actually found the identity and comfort he had craved.
- Difficult life choices of loved ones change our interactions and family dynamics. It becomes a challenge to know how to adjust to the transitions left in the wake.
- Loss of a loved one changes nearly every aspect of life. What once felt good and secure can quickly turn into a fog of loneliness.

I don't mean to bring you down with this list, but often, awareness of the heavy load of "transition baggage" we carry can lead us toward the curl of the wave. Mourning must break, for morning to break. Thankfully, the Scriptures teach us how to lament. I not only didn't want to do this, but I didn't know how.

Vulnerability and Songs of Lament

David, in his songs, teaches us lament. Not only does he teach us the value of vulnerability through expressing pain, but he also teaches us the importance of music and poetry in our lives. We can become so busy that the arts, God's gifts of creativity, find no place in our lives.

We need music and art to mourn well. They help us paint pictures of our emotions that words can't express. They go beyond rational, scientific thinking to the core "feeling channels" of our hearts. Imagine watching a movie with no soundtrack. You would miss so much. Transitioning without music and art leaves us without a soundtrack. God created harmony throughout his creation. Music is everywhere and will help us lament, find comfort, and find joy once again. Make a playlist. Get out in nature. Hear the birds. Listen to the wind and feel it on your face. Cry with the setting sun.

Walter Bruggeman, in his book on Psalms, traces the movement of lament and life through seasons of orientation when things are stable, to disorientation when life falls apart or changes, and then on to reorientation, where one finds peace in transition. I find this a helpful tool, and we can follow the psalms through each of these stages, except for a few such as Psalm 88. In this psalm, the songwriter does not yet reach reorientation and is "just being real" in despair. Sometimes we get stuck, and our journey takes a bit longer than we wish. I will share a journal excerpt that is included in my book *Wednesdays with Wyndham,* written during the starkest and darkest transition in my life to date.

Transitions Hit Hard

Though I knew the day would come, I always longed for the day to be another day, not this one. But the day came. I said goodbye (for now) to my beloved Wyndham on November 21, 2019. I am grateful for every day and every extra day that God gave us. Two days before he died, I got to hear Wyndham's voice again, loud and clear. He told me clearly that he was going to die and that he loved me. We exchanged precious words of love. I assured him he would live on in me and in us, and I would love him forever. I tried to find some way to thank him for his love and his life. I reassured him we would be okay. This special time was a gift.

The next day he could not eat and was exceedingly tired, with a fever. His nurse thought he could possibly rebound, since he had in March, but that we would know in a few days. That night, Leigh Ann brought the three little Shaw girls over to hug Papa, at Emery's insistence. Sam was out of town on a business trip. The girls beautifully sang for him, "Amazing Grace," "Twinkle Little Star," "Jesus Loves Me," and "He's Got the Whole World in His Hands," the last song with verses including every member of our family, including all the dogs.

This was a gift that comforted him and brought him joy on what we did not know would be his last evening on earth. Later that night, Melissa, Kevin, and Kristen arrived, and we talked to him and prayed, cried, and laughed. Wyndham seemed to enjoy listening, though he could not respond except to squeeze his eyes. Our son, Sam, made arrangements to fly back.

The next morning Sam arrived, and we all sat with Wyndham, unsure of what to expect. We sat with him and loved him with all that was within us. I had begged God that morning to be kind to Wyndham and to us in his passing, and he was. Wyndham was not in pain and the transition was fast. Our hearts broke for us but rejoiced for him as he exited this world with impeccable courage, gratitude, faith, and love. I could even see some cheerfulness before he passed, as his eyes smiled. I know that eye-smile. He had no voice, but eyes and ears. Since we still thought there was more time, I made a run to the drugstore to get a needed medical supply, and Kristen and Sam went for a prayer walk. Melissa and Kevin stayed with him. Jacob was nearby, attentive to the needs. As a family, we have been on this journey together, all in.

As soon as I walked out the door, Wyndham was gone, likely thinking of protecting me, once again. When I walked to him it was clear his body was vacant, a mere shell that once housed the spiritual being that still lives. For this certain hope, I give thanks to God.

The world felt dizzying that day and many days after. The tears kept flowing, though accompanied by smiles and precious memories. I feel strangely both sad and grateful. It feels weird to be able to just walk out my door to go somewhere, and I find myself feeling guilty for being able to do so. That probably makes little sense, but many things feel a little strange right now. Transitions are hard. That dreaded day also brought many precious, touching moments, which are ours to treasure. There were also some moments that one day will give us laughter, but not yet.

The following day, when the hospital bed and medical equipment were all gone, our dog, Denver, walked into our room and just stood there as if frozen, looking around as if he were thinking, "Everything is different. What do I do now?" I felt the same.

Job Demonstrates Lament

In the biblical account of Job, we find a man attacked by the evil one, suffering intensely. In a matter of days, his whole world fell apart. Job was a man of integrity who knew God and whom God knew. They trusted each other. Job's responses to the extreme transitions that brought great suffering teach us to be honest with God. Gut-level honest. He did not hold back expressing to God and his friends how he felt, while at the same time he knew God was God, and he was not. He also had a keen sense of his own identity, in that he held to his convictions and never lost his integrity. He had questions for God that God did not answer, which I admit I don't yet understand. I am struck by Job's lament to God in Job 10:1–10 (emphasis added). This, my friends, is a snapshot of lament. Job holds to his God-given identity even though he loathes the day he was born. He also tells God that God doesn't understand him because God is not human.

> "I loathe my very life;
> therefore I will give free rein to my complaint
> and speak out in the bitterness of my soul.

I say to God: Do not declare me guilty,
but tell me what charges you have against me.

Does it please you to oppress me,
to spurn the work of your hands,
while you smile on the plans of the wicked?

Do you have eyes of flesh?
Do you see as a mortal sees?

Are your days like those of a mortal
or your years like those of a strong man,

that you must search out my faults
and probe after my sin—

though you know that I am not guilty
and that no one can rescue me from your hand?

"Your hands shaped me and made me.
Will you now turn and destroy me?

Remember that you molded me like clay.
Will you now turn me to dust again?

Did you not pour me out like milk
and curdle me like cheese?"

I can't help but wonder if God thought of Job's words nearly six hundred years later when he became flesh and dwelt among us in the form of Jesus. Now he had eyes of flesh and saw as mortals see. He would become acquainted with human grief. God had such compassion that he lowered himself to feel and experience such humanity. This is love.

Job named his physical and emotional pain as he described in detail his suffering, loathing the day he was born. He did this out loud, because it was recorded for all to know. I believe he sets us an example of an *honest relationship* with God. Relationships require honesty and vulnerability, yet we can become expert "stuffers" before God, thinking he does not want to hear. What kind of relationship withholds vulnerability?

Giving Lament Words

In lament, putting our hurt into words with God—perhaps even our hurt *toward* God—helps us get in touch with what is really going on in our hearts. Often, it is when I try to describe my pain in prayer to God or when sharing or praying with a friend that I get in touch with my emotions, and the tears flow. It is hard to go there, because it feels weak and vulnerable, and it tempts me to feel I should be stronger. *In Getting Your Life Back,* John Eldredge challenges readers to name things in prayer: "Come into this hurt, this feeling of abandonment, this numbness...or whatever stands in the way of intimacy. But decide, 'I will here, in this, love you.'"[13] This seems a helpful practice. Can you name your emotions to God, or do you tend to deal with him concerning facts? Try naming your fear, insecurity, loneliness, anger, and hurt. Only then will you also be able to name your joy, comfort, security, gratitude, laughter, and healing.

Lamenting Transitions

Transitional life circumstances bring on transitioning emotions. While it would be nice to be able to immediately feel, *What a wonderful opportunity this new situation brings me,* this doesn't often happen in real life. Several transitions I've faced and already mentioned (such as moves, loss of loved ones, caregiving, and job changes) have brought on great feelings of loss, fear, insecurity, hurt, and all kinds of other emotions. Usually, I felt somewhat numb and disoriented at first. Then the whole "grief gang" would come calling—bringing all the named stages of grief: denial, anger, bargaining, and so much more. Grief has stages, but they don't proceed in an orderly fashion. A line in the sad movie *The Rabbit Hole* aptly describes the weight of loss as "like a brick in your pocket." You reach in (your pocket) and it's always there. But eventually...it's okay. Eventually, mine has become sort of okay. I am left with rich memories, deeper experiences, and a closer walk with God; but on any day, I can notice that brick in my pocket. A few weeks ago, my dog got extremely sick from an abscessed tooth and

---

13. John Eldredge, *Get Your Life Back: Everyday Practices for a World Gone Mad* (Nashville, TN: Nelson, 2020), 99.

pancreatitis. Thankfully, he fully recovered, but when I got to the front desk of my new vet's office (I had never met her since I had just moved) and told them my dog was sick, I fell apart, weeping uncontrollably. You see, Denver sat under Wyndham's hospital bed every day as I sat beside the bed. Denver is now my only roommate. Bricks were flying that day. That poor veterinarian must have thought I was a little overdramatic. Grief often surprises us.

We may find ourselves grieving over transitions that are good things, things we have long desired. While parents raise their children to become independent and successful human beings, it can be hard when that goal becomes reality and they leave home. Many of life's day-to-day activities in our younger years were centered around our children. Then, suddenly, there are no more sports events to attend, no more school activities, and teens no longer hang out at our house. After our kids went off to college, I remember crying in several aisles in the grocery store, thinking of all the "favorites" I used to purchase for them. We find we need to relearn activities, such as how to prepare meals for two (or one if you are single). Many couples go through challenging transitions as they learn how to find or rekindle the affection and attention that previous demands on their time kept them from nourishing. It takes work and naming the emotions the transitions bring to understand ourselves and each other.

Grieving—OK and Necessary

Grieving is part of God's plan—so it's not only okay, but necessary. Lament takes intentional time and effort. It is hard work, but as God's image bearers we are meant to grieve. God grieves, and God rejoices. We experience emotions because we are made in his image. We know that Jesus wept, and we likely even memorized that short verse in the Scriptures. He mourned, he grieved. In the Bible, grieving was accompanied by visceral activities such as fasting, tearing clothes, wearing ashes, singing songs of mourning, and crying loudly. I have punched many a pillow as I have lamented. Eventually, mourners find rest for their souls by turning to God and deepening their faith. The psalms of despair have silver linings—"But God." When we find ourselves in the crashing waves, staggering and going under, we need to remember that God will hold us tightly.

Yet I am always with you;
you hold me by my right hand.

You guide me with your counsel,
and afterward you will take me into glory.

Whom have I in heaven but you?
And earth has nothing I desire besides you.

My flesh and my heart may fail,
but God is the strength of my heart

What Now, God?

and my portion forever. (Psalm 73:23–26)

While the above scripture is faith building and comforting, the scriptures that precede these show the heart struggle to get to this place of trust. Notice that the psalmist was not afraid to vulnerably express his struggle.

But as for me, my feet had almost slipped;
  I had nearly lost my foothold.
For I envied the arrogant
  when I saw the prosperity of the wicked.

They have no struggles;
  their bodies are healthy and strong.

They are free from common human burdens;
  they are not plagued by human ills…

Surely in vain have I kept my heart pure
  And have I washed my hands in innocence.

All day long I have been afflicted,
  and every morning
 brings new punishments.
  If I had spoken out like that,
I would have betrayed your children.

When I tried to understand all this,
  it troubled me deeply
till I entered the sanctuary of God. (Psalm 73:2–5, 13–17a)

Keep going until you enter the sanctuary of God. This sanctuary is not a church auditorium, but the safe, strong hand of God.

Lament Requires Desert Journeys

The ancient mystic John of the Cross put to words the heart laments we suffer as he wrote of "the dark night of the soul." These dark nights describe the disorientation in our lives, the times we feel our souls wandering in the desert. This "time in the desert" happens again and again with God's people. Whether forty years or forty days, wilderness or desert, dark nights of the soul should not surprise us. They are a normal part of the Christian journey.

Author John Eldredge recounts that in the Gospels, it was the transition times when the disciples got to have Jesus to themselves. The intimacy was in those moments.[14] We need times with Jesus to transition well. Our souls need transition times.

Eldridge continues, explaining our need to slow down to transition well:

> We are forcing our souls through multiple gear changes each day, each *hour*, and after years of this we aren't even sure what to say when a friend genuinely inquires, 'How are you?' We don't really know; we aren't sure what we feel anymore. We live at one speed: go. All the subtleties of human experience have been forced into one state of being."[15]

---

14. Eldredge, *Get Your Life Back*, 72.
15. Eldredge, *Get Your Life Back*, 67.

What Now, God?

Remember the three-mile-an-hour God? If we are rushing through life, how can we hope to transition well?

Transitions not only involve our life situations but also mental and spiritual challenges to our faith and belief systems. Why do we believe what we believe? We must answer these questions at various times in our lives. During the challenging past couple of years, not only has the world faced a pandemic, but the United States has encountered deep political division and racial unrest. After the recent and publicized unjust murders of several Black men and women, I further educated myself with some books that poignantly describe the systemic racism in our history. These accounts were left out of my history books when I was growing up years ago. I felt stunned and horrified concerning things I had been wrongly taught or that had been left untaught, much of which I was sadly, ashamedly unaware of. This rocked me.

During this same time, my years of studies concerning the role of women in the church brought questions concerning interpretation that I had never previously had the courage to ask or confront. I had stuffed my questions without digging into them through my study of the Scriptures—I was afraid to dig deeper. These types of encounters bring on various kinds of transitions and require that we "work out [our] salvation with fear and trembling" (Philippians 2:12). I don't think this means I need to be afraid to work things out, but in the context of the scripture I must remember that it is our good and mighty God who laid his life down for me as a servant—

this is the Lord I seek to serve and apprentice.

I have needed, but not particularly enjoyed, times in my figurative deserts to uncomfortably wrestle with my questions and thoughts. In case any of you are worrying about me, I have not gone anywhere. I believe with all my heart in our one Lord, one faith, one baptism, one God and Father of us all—and the Bible is more amazing to me than ever. Though I have deep convictions, I am continually learning and some things I understand differently than I once did. This is a good thing. I grow and learn. I also believe that God intends for us to be in a spiritual community, and I love my church family. Our families will never be perfect, but they should be a safe place to question and grow. I learned several decades ago that I had to be honest with what I believe, what I felt veered from God's plans, and what I had questions about. We all go through our journeys, and if you haven't, you will. Journeys are not only okay, but they are necessary. Becoming a Christian is not a one-and-done lifestyle. I must both engage myself and be engaged with others whose grief, lament, and transitions bring change to their lives. In the desert I have learned to experience a deeper, more tangible relationship with God that moves beyond function.

Like Jacob wrestling with the angel of God, at times we must wrestle to find our deepest convictions and beliefs. Growth means transition. While we can stand on solid convictions from the Scriptures, the presuppositions we bring to the table mean our thoughts are not always neat and tidy, and shame on me if I think I have learned all I need to learn. The Psalms remind us of what we do not know.

Become a Songwriter

If you have never done so, I encourage you during transitions to write your own psalms to God. You need not show them to anyone, but the process itself may prove helpful. I believe this is one reason we have the Psalms. Not only do the writers' songs express their emotions, but they elicit ours as we get our souls wrapped around them. God knows we need to emote, so please "psalm away."

Honestly, some of my times of deepest lament have been the times when I most closely felt the hand of God. While I don't want to experience the suffering, in strange ways I almost miss that indescribable intimacy, when there are no words to be found. Many times I was without words, just sitting with God as he sat with me.

When we grieve and the tears flow, our hearts go through many workouts. As they empty, they also grow with more room to expand. I share an excerpt from a writing from Adam Birr after his wife passed away from cancer, leaving behind a broken heart and their young children. No matter the transitions we face, we can gain much truth from his observations and experience.

Make Space for Lament
By Adam Birr
Glasgow, Scotland

Kirstie's death started the final phase of grief. This was the time when most people started to grieve for her, but I was already four and a half years into this journey. I knew I had been grieving during those years, and I discovered I did not need to grieve again the things I had grieved during the previous phases. I remember that several months before she died, I grieved the fact that I would not buy any new clothes for her again. It felt sad at the time to have this husband activity taken away from me. After she passed, I was in a local supermarket (it was during the first COVID-19 lockdown, and supermarkets were the only shops open), and as I walked past the women's clothing aisles, I was tempted to feel sad, but I told myself that I didn't need to feel sad as I had already grieved this several months prior. Nothing had changed in this regard because she had passed. Not everyone feels this way, but this helped me. Grief, however, did not go away.

Many people tend to think that grief diminishes over time, like this black ball in a jar.

What Now, God?

But the reality is very different. The grief doesn't diminish. Soldiers who were on the Normandy D-Day beaches, when they recall their stories, suffer grief just as much today as they did in 1944. The grief doesn't fade into nothing as if it were a car driving into the sunset along a straight desert road. It is just there and always will be. A big ball of blackness in the jar of life.

You can't move on from this. The black ball of grief remains. The ball doesn't change, but the jar can. We can grow around the grief. The jar can get bigger.

As hard as we try, we cannot move on from grief, but we can move forward. As a widower with four children, the need to move forward is paramount and not optional. I must move forward.

Reflections on Identity

- Life moves rapidly, tempting us to forego needed time to mourn transitions. Have you taken time to mourn, or do you tend to push through because grief is messy and hard? Do you feel guilty or selfish for mourning, thinking you should be stronger? Consider planning a time to intentionally lament transitions and losses.

- Remember, relationships require honesty and vulnerability. Reflect on ways you stuff what you feel, thinking perhaps God does not want to hear about it, that he doesn't care, or that you are not worth his time? What might change your view?

- Do you believe it is okay to put your hurt into words with God—or perhaps even express your hurt toward God? Try writing or praying your hurt concerning a transition you have had to face. Name your emotions (your fear, insecurity, loneliness, shame, anger, and hurt) to God. Practice vulnerability. Only when we do that, will we be able to also name our joy, comfort, security, gratitude, laughter, and healing.

- Sometimes, we can feel like there is no coexistence possible for doubt, confusion, anger and faith. The Psalms teach us otherwise. Try reading several Psalms through the eyes of orientation, disorientation, and reorientation. Do you feel like it is okay to experience times of disorientation?

- With a troubling transition on your mind, try writing a psalm that emotes your true heart. How might this help you to reorient?

Chapter 3:
Walking Through Candyland

It's important that we don't rush through the orientation, disorientation, and reorientation cycle. In many transitions, we want to get to the end of disorientation quickly. But when we rush, we circumvent a God-given process.

Years ago, when my children were young, we played an occasional game of Candyland. To be honest, I played as occasionally as they would allow. For parents, this game requires great patience and love, as the monotony can make you want to poke your eyes out. In this game, depending on which color card you draw, you can advance, take shortcuts, get caught in forest swamps, or even get stuck in licorice. Just when you round the corner to get home for the win, some strange piece of candy is bent on defeating you, sending you back to the beginning. Navigating transitions can resemble Candyland. Steps forward, steps backward, delays, and traps. Stuck in swamps. But all the while, we can't forget that candy surrounds us. It just seems quite hard to taste it.

Thankfully, we aren't meant to live in the desert forever, nor in Candyland. God desires for us to find our way home, for us to enjoy the taste of goodness, and for our senses to experience him in ever-increasing ways. But how do we do that? Hagar is one of my favorite people in the Bible. She faced huge transitions, most of which were decided for her. In her Candyland journey, she often got sent back and then fell into traps, but she finally learned to taste the candy. Let's travel with Hagar through several of her transitions.

Hagar in the Desert

Hagar knew the desert, and she knew grief. Two times she mourned in the desert, and her tears are the first ones recorded in the Bible.[16] She was not the favored wife of Abraham but instead was Sarah's servant. Sarah gave Hagar to Abraham in the most intimate way while trying to "help God" keep his promise to Abraham. When Hagar became pregnant, bitterness and rivalry ensued between the women, causing Hagar to run away to the desert. She returned to Sarah per God's request, but when Sarah finally gave birth and the promised son, Isaac, was weaned, Hagar's son, Ishmael, taunted the boy. In reaction, Sarah sent Hagar and Ishmael away with only some food and water that Abraham had given. In the desert again, Hagar mourned for her son who was dying under a bush after their supplies ran out. How used, rejected, and disposable she must have felt. In the Genesis account of her life, Hagar cycled through times of orientation, disorientation, and reorientation and could have scripted Psalm 13.

---

16. Debbie Blue, "The Other Woman," *The Christian Century*, November 24, 2014.

What Now, God?

How long, LORD? Will you forget me forever?
*   How long will you hide your face from me?*

How long must I wrestle with my thoughts
*   and day after day have sorrow in my heart?*
*   How long will my enemy triumph over me?*

Look on me and answer, LORD my God.
*   Give light to my eyes, or I will sleep in death,*
and my enemy will say, "I have overcome him,"
*   and my foes will rejoice when I fall.*

But I trust in your unfailing love;
*   my heart rejoices in your salvation.*

I will sing the LORD's praise,
*   for he has been good to me.*

When You Can't Choose Your Transitions

Genesis 21:9–21 records the dramatic unfolding of events in Hagar's life. Though Hagar had come from the socially and politically advanced country of Egypt, her status as a maidservant and foreigner gave her a disadvantage among Hebrew women.

Though a maidservant's role was not the same as that of chattel slavery, Hagar legally "belonged" to Sarah. Some interpreters speculate that Abraham's gifts of menservants and maidservants from Egypt (Genesis 12:16) may have brought Hagar to them. Though we do not know how this arrangement began, the Scriptures make it clear that Hagar answered to Sarah, not Abraham (Genesis 16:6).

Hagar, as Sarah's maidservant, received a great "promotion" when Sarah had Abraham take her to become a sort of surrogate mother for her. Though the Bible does not describe Hagar's emotions at this time, perhaps she felt like a person who won a lottery. For a woman in Hagar's position, bearing the child of a leader would be an honor, raise her social status, and make her a concubine, or secondary wife. She might eventually look forward to being the mother of the tribe's leader, making her a "queen" of sorts. Perhaps Hagar found a time of orientation as her lot in life changed, seemingly for the good. However, this time of orientation would quickly change to disorientation.

When Life Stinks and Isn't Fair

Hagar became pregnant with Abraham's son, not by her choice but by Sarah's insistence. The Bible is not clear as to the details of what happened between Sarah and Hagar, but Sarah felt that Hagar despised her after Hagar became pregnant. In reaction, Sarah began to mistreat Hagar to the point that Hagar felt the need to run away (Genesis 16:1–8). The orientation time of pregnancy and exalted status likely felt short-lived for Hagar. She became a disoriented runaway in the desert until an angel of God approached her, calling her by her name and asking her, "Where have you come from, and where are you going?" These poignant questions are important to answer during any season of disorientation or transition. We must determine where we have come from and where we are going. (Remember John 13:3?) God tells Hagar to go back to Sarah and says that he will increase her descendants; yet, with that good news, he also delivers some not-so-encouraging news. The angel tells her that her son will live in hostility toward his brothers (Genesis 16:9–12).

Her disorientation turns to reorientation when she realizes that in her misery and distress, God *saw* her. Hagar is the only person in the Bible who gives a name to God, as she names him *El Roi,* the God who sees. Genesis 16:13 illustrates an important aspect of reorientation as Hagar states, "I have now seen the One who sees me." To reorient, we must see God.

Just When I Thought I Was Reoriented

For the next thirteen years, as Ishmael grows, life goes well for Hagar. She is now part of the family of Abraham, having mothered the son of one who would be the father of many nations. The Scriptures do not give many details of Hagar's life during this time, but there is no record of her leaving or being disoriented. After waiting for many years, God fulfills the promise originally given to Abraham and Sarah that they would bear a son. Isaac is born, and after he is weaned, Hagar's son Ishmael begins to taunt him. Once again, Sarah is angry, and as a protective and perhaps jealous mama, she sends Hagar away. Hagar does not seem to remember the name she had previously given God, "the One who sees." Genesis records Hagar's difficult, disorienting situation.

> But Sarah saw that the son whom Hagar the Egyptian had borne to Abraham was mocking, and she said to Abraham, "Get rid of that slave woman and her son, for that woman's son will never share in the inheritance with my son Isaac."
>
> The matter distressed Abraham greatly because it concerned his son.
>
> But God said to him, "Do not be so distressed about the boy and your slave woman. Listen to whatever Sarah tells you, because it is through Isaac that your offspring will be reckoned.
>
> I will make the son of the slave into a nation also, because he is your offspring."
>
> Early the next morning Abraham took some food and a skin of water and gave them to Hagar. He set them on her shoulders and then sent her off with the boy. She went on her way and wandered in the Desert of Beersheba.
>
> When the water in the skin was gone, she put the boy under one of the bushes.
>
> Then she went off and sat down about a bowshot away, for she thought, "I cannot watch the boy die." And as she sat there, she began to sob. (Genesis 21:9–16)

The Cycle Repeats

Hagar loved her son yet felt helpless to help him. She had not asked for her situation. After they wandered in the desert again, their water ran out. Ishmael was dying, and life felt cruel and unfair. She kept her distance because she could not bear to watch her son die (v. 16). She did the opposite of "leaning in" to his needs; she leaned away. She kept her distance, probably to protect her emotions. Some scholars perceive her as a harsh, unloving woman, but this does not seem consistent with her pain at the thought of losing Ishmael. Rather, she portrays a woman broken in despair.

Once again, Hagar is seen mourning in the desert. According to Israel's social standards, the desert was the least desirable place. In some traditions, the desert was "further conceptualized as a place of nonexistence and thus as the abode of the dead."[17] Have you ever felt that you lived in the desert? Do you feel you are there now?

Hagar Could Sing This Psalm

The first four verses of Psalm 13 well reflect Hagar's time in the desert, sobbing, unable to find the face of God. The God "who sees" could not be seen.

> *How long, LORD? Will you forget me forever?*
> *How long will you hide your face from me?*
>
> *How long must I wrestle with my thoughts*
> *and day after day have sorrow in my heart?*
> *How long will my enemy triumph over me?*

---

17. A. Haldar, *The Notion of the Desert in Sumero-Accadian and West-Semitic Religions* (Uppsala: Lundequistska Bokhandeln, 1950), 14. Cited in https://www-oxfordscholarship-com.ezproxy.regent.edu/view/10.1093/oso/9780198745327.001.0001/oso-9780198745327, accessed June 28, 2020.

Look on me and answer, LORD my God.
Give light to my eyes, or I will sleep in death,
and my enemy will say, "I have overcome him,
and my foes will rejoice when I fall.

Once again, Hagar felt hopeless and mistreated. She drew the wrong Candyland card and was sent back. The God who had once seen her had suddenly been blinded, according to her thoughts. I can only imagine her anguish in running out of water, forced to let her beloved son die. Hagar's anguish felt intense. How she must have wrestled with thoughts of injustice and abandonment by God, Abraham, and Sarah. Once her family, Abraham and Sarah now felt like enemies. Who but an enemy could treat one as a prisoner of war, marching them toward death? From Hagar's view, her enemies had triumphed.

Having earlier named God when she said, "I have now seen the One who sees me" (Genesis 16:13), the light is now gone from Hagar's eyes. Psalm 13:3 expresses a longing for light in the eyes, but darkness prevails. The psalm mirrors Hagar in the desert, waiting for Ishmael to die.

Citing historian Gary Ebersole's essay on ritual weeping and its function, Old Testament scholar Ekaterina Kozlova studies Hagar, opining that "Genesis 21 showcases the power of ritual weeping not only in opposing the breakdown of a social system but also in advancing its restoration."[18] Hagar's lament in the desert prepares her for verses 5 and 6 in Psalm 13, as she once again cycles toward reorientation.

> *But I trust in your unfailing love;*
> *my heart rejoices in your salvation.*
>
> *I will sing the LORD's praise,*
> *for he has been good to me.*

As Hagar vulnerably laments her abandonment in the desert, God helps her gain reorientation as once again she sees the God who sees her. This time though, she hears the God who hears her.

Reoriented

As Hagar sat sobbing, a bowshot away from her dying son, God helped her see him once again. Genesis 21:17–21 reminds us that in one's darkest hour, God sees, and he hears.

> *God heard the boy crying, and the angel of God called to Hagar from heaven and said to her, "What is the matter, Hagar? Do not be afraid; God has heard the boy crying as he lies there.*
> *Lift the boy up and take him by the hand, for I will make him into a great nation."*

---

18. Ekaterina E. Kozlova, *Maternal Grief in the Hebrew Bible*, Oxford Scholarship Online, June 17, 2017, https://www-oxfordscholarship-com.ezproxy.regent.edu/view/10.1093/oso/9780198796879.001.0001/oso-9780198796879-chapter-2, 2.

> *Then God opened her eyes and she saw a well of water. So she went and filled the skin with water and gave the boy a drink.*
>
> *God was with the boy as he grew up. He lived in the desert and became an archer. While he was living in the Desert of Paran, his mother got a wife for him from Egypt.*

We Need Deserts, and We Need Wells

In this second encounter with God, the well that could quench Ishmael's and Hagar's thirst was not visible to Hagar while she was in distress; yet the same God who saw her continued to see her and hear her cries. God sees and hears us, but we do not always see and hear him. Her eyes had to be opened to see God's provision for her. She had lost sight of the well where God had seen her.

These two "well encounters" may be near the same place.[19] In both encounters, God saw and heard Hagar's pain. In both encounters, her heart and eyes were opened to God's loving care for her. When her eyes are opened, she encounters God, who tells her not to be afraid and to "lift the boy up and take him by the hand, for I will make him into a great nation." Her reorientation with God also brought restoration to her relationship with her son. Reorientation often brings healing to stressed relationships.

---

19. It is possible that both encounters with God at the well are at the same well. Beersheba was a desert region, as was Shur. Both were on the way to Egypt. E.H. Plumptre, *The Bible Educator, Vol 1* (London: Cassell Petter and Galpin, 1877), 174. 101.h.184.

What Now, God?

In her article, "The Other Woman," Debbie Blue notes the parallel between Hagar's story and Abraham's story. Hagar takes Ishmael into the desert for imminent death until an angel of God shows her a well. Abraham takes Isaac to Mount Moriah where death seems sure until an angel speaks and shows him a ram. Blue further notes something many scholars think likely. After Sarah dies, Abraham marries Keturah. "According to Midrashic tradition, 'Keturah' is actually Hagar's real name—'Hagar,' the 'other' is just a description"[20]. Blue conjectures as she continues, "So Abraham doesn't cut off the counternarrative. He embraces it, takes it into his heart. He lies in bed with it—makes love with Hagar again."[21]

Hagar's life reminds us that God hears and knows the distress of his children, no matter what happens. He cares, always. Even if God had not provided the well and Ishmael had died, the story would not have been over, because there is eternal life for those who belong to God. However, for this purpose, God would have Ishmael live. God was keeping a promise. He always does.

> *For your kingdom is an everlasting kingdom.*
> *You rule throughout all generations.*
> *The LORD always keeps his promises;*
> *he is gracious in all he does.*

---

20. Tamar Kadari, "Keturah: Midrash and Aggadah," *The Encyclopedia of Jewish Women*, https://jwa.org/encyclopedia/article/keturah-midrash-and-aggadah.

21. Debbie Blue, "The Other Woman," https://www.christiancentury.org/article/2014-11/other-woman.

The LORD helps the fallen
  and lifts those bent beneath their loads.
(Psalm 145:13–14 NLT)

Hagar's transformation took place when her eyes were opened and she saw a well of water. Had that well always been there? We do not know, but we do know that God provided what was needed. For me, transformation takes place when I believe that God sees, hears, and cares, even when his answers are not as I wish. Transformation comes when my eyes are open to see what God is providing for me, no matter how painful the situation. He always provides through his Spirit what is humanly impossible. When I open my eyes to see God (Ephesians 1:17), like Hagar, I find the well of living water that God has so graciously supplied. I must trust his love.

> *But I trust in your unfailing love;*
>   *my heart rejoices in your salvation.*
>
> *I will sing the LORD's praise,*
>   *for he has been good to me.* (Psalm 13:5–6)

I can think of few men and women of God described in the Bible who did not spend time in the desert. Adam and Eve had to leave the garden. Abraham wandered in the desert, and Moses in the wilderness, Hagar spent time in the desert, Naomi wandered back to her homeland. And these are only a few of the desert dwellers.

What Now, God?

Jesus went to the wilderness immediately after his baptism and before beginning his ministry. We can easily forget that Paul spent three years in the desert after his conversion and before beginning his ministry to the Gentiles. Why spend time in the desert? For most, it seems the desert allowed them to wrestle with who they were and who God is. They learned to transition with God. If we feel we are in the desert, we have good company there.

Choices in the Desert

As transitions carry us back and forth across Candyland terrain, it is important to remember that while we don't always get to choose transitions, we do have a choice while journeying through them. We may have to find God again. We can always find our way home when we choose to love and be loved.

Close your eyes and hear the song of birds, the snowfall, the rolling waves. Hear the urging of his Spirit as God moves in your heart. Smell the fragrance of the honeysuckle and the falling leaves. Touch the skin of a newborn baby or put your toes in rushing water as you feel its caress. Feel the wind on your face. Watch the sunrise and sunset, the wildflowers in the wind, and the star-laden night sky. Feel the warmth of love down deep in your soul. Breathe in and taste the goodness of God. God made our senses and longs to inhabit each of them. Make the time to see, hear, taste, smell, and touch. On purpose. And stand in awe.

In all transitions:
>We can notice the good in people.
>We can be thankful.
>We can pray.
>We can meditate on what is true, trustworthy, worthy of praise, honorable, pure, and lovely.
>We can hope.
>We can imagine being with God forever.
>We can laugh and cry, mourn and lament.
>We can feel.
>We can hear the words of God.
>We can pray some more.
>We may even see a goose or an eagle.
>Or a message from God through a friend.

And in the desert, we will be given a well. We must simply trust that God will provide it.

> *Who shall separate us from the love of Christ? Shall trouble or hardship or persecution or famine or nakedness or danger or sword?*
>
> *As it is written:*
>> *"For your sake we face death all day long;*
>> *we are considered as sheep to be slaughtered."*
>
> *No, in all these things we are more than conquerors through him who loved us.*
>
> *For I am convinced that neither death nor life, neither angels nor demons, neither the present nor the future, nor any powers,*

What Now, God?

neither height nor depth, nor anything else in all creation, will be able to separate us from the love of God that is in Christ Jesus our Lord. (Romans 8:35–39)

The Message version states these last verses this way:

I'm absolutely convinced that nothing—nothing living or dead, angelic or demonic, today or tomorrow,
high or low, thinkable or unthinkable—absolutely nothing can get between us and God's love because of the way that Jesus our Master has embraced us.

Pairing Grief and Gratitude
By Judy McCreary
Wasilla, Alaska

Some transitions are planned, prepared for, and anticipated; others come out of nowhere, an unexpected and seemingly cruel turn of events in life that leaves you in a place you didn't choose. My entire family faced unexpected transitions all at once. Four years ago, if I had been told how much my life would transition, I never would have believed it.

My wonderful husband of thirty years was killed in 2018 on his way home from work, hit by a distracted driver. It was violent and sudden. How one processes transition seems to depend greatly on a variety of factors, and my kids and I have all wrestled with it in our own ways. When Pete first died, finding my footing amid crushing pain seemed impossible, but my four kids needed a mom who was not falling apart. I sought grief and trauma counseling and did the work.

Our oldest was twenty-two, newly married, and had recently moved to Boston. She read books on grief, looked introspectively, talked, and talked some more. She knew she needed to build close friendships, and she needed them quickly. Our second, in the middle of college, is the one who learns most easily through experience, and for parents this is sometimes scary. You must let go of control and let them learn for themselves. Though I offered love and encouragement, in the end she had to sort out her relationship with God on her own. Marvelously, she did. Our high school girl secured two jobs right after the accident. Self-protection and bottling up emotions became second nature to her. It has taken time, but different life experiences, including dating, have drawn out the self she was protecting for so long. My high school son is still on his journey, but he is a fighter. Transitioning from losing a father as a thirteen-year-old boy is hard.

I prayed, often asking God, "What's next?" I began a conscious reconstruction of my life. In theory, there is something amazing about the chance to create a new life—unless the one you had was the only one you wanted. I now had to make decisions without Pete. He wasn't there, and the choices were now mine alone. What color should I paint the family room? Should I sell part of our business? Should I take this trip? Should I move?

After much prayer, in late June 2021, my two youngest kids and I packed our dogs into the hatchback of the Subaru, followed the U-Haul, and set off on the sixty-five-hour drive from Cincinnati to Anchorage. It took us nine days, and it was a magnificent journey through the Canadian Rockies and British Columbia. We all entered new jobs and roles, a new church, new relationships, new city, and new climate. I had never experienced minus 20-degree weather! And while I'm living in the most beautiful place I have ever seen and am loving our new church family, I still miss my friends of more than thirty years and our shared history. We transitioned through so much of life together—birth and adoption of children, marriage, job changes, church challenges, loss of children, loss of parents and spouses, empty nesting, launching children, children getting baptized, and children struggling to find their faith.

My girls are now moving confidently into adulthood. All but one live in Alaska. This is an infinite blessing. I realize my role as a mother is changing, and my impending empty nest is looking different from the way I imagined it. Without exception, life transitions, even when positive, contain a component of grief.

When we adopted our son from the Philippines, we were told

that although he was going home to his forever family, he would grieve. To form a healthy attachment, he had to grieve the loss of what was familiar, even though the change brought new and wonderful things. We all must do the same.

I have changed. I am more comfortable expressing my opinion. I care less about what people think, and hopefully I am more compassionate. I pray more and control less. Scriptures that barely resonated with me before are now huge in my growing understanding of God and his nature. And the father-son talk a dad often has with the boy who wants to marry his daughter? Well, if you need help with that, I'm your girl! I've stumbled through that conversation twice on my own now and have gotten pretty comfortable with it.

I believe God helps smooth our journeys toward peace, humility, and gratitude through life transitions as we understand that he is the God who also suffers and who loves us passionately. Praying vulnerably, and intentionally embracing gratefulness morning and evening, help me capture my thoughts and set them on things above. I'm at the point where I can allow gratitude for God's miracles to coexist with unimaginable grief. It's a big life, embracing all that. God has enabled me to widen my lens. Where once all I could see was sadness and fear, I can now also cradle the beauty in God's miracles. It has taken time. It won't happen in an afternoon or with one decision.

Can we find peace with the unanswered questions of life? To embrace the future while honoring the past requires gratitude and grief. Both, fully felt, are powerful side by side.

My daughter Ryan once wrote: *What was your dad like?*

This question rarely comes, and only does when people are not afraid to ask. I smile and whisper, *That…is my favorite question.*

Reflections on Identity

- Hagar experienced devastating transitions beyond her control. She named God *El Roi,* the God who sees. What difference does it make during difficult transition to believe that God sees you, and cares?

- Hagar could well relate to the words written in Psalm 13. Read this Psalm with orientation, disorientation, and reorientation in mind as you reflect on a difficult transition in your life. Reflect on "wells" that God has provided for you during times of distress.

- Reflect on the words, "As transitions carry us back and forth across Candyland terrain, it is important to remember that while we don't always get to choose transitions, we do have a choice while journeying through them. We may have to find God again." We can always find our way home when we choose to accept God's love. Reflect on choices you have made as you have journeyed through transitions. Have they led you closer to God or farther from him? If we believe God sees, hears, and cares, we will more quickly run to him. Reflect on times you have experienced the God who sees and hears. The God who cares.

- Bring to mind a time when you experienced awe. What was it like? As the chapter states, "Close your eyes and hear the song of birds, the snowfall, the rolling waves. Hear the urging of his Spirit as God moves in your heart. Smell the fragrance of the honeysuckle and the falling leaves. Touch the skin of a newborn baby or put your toes in rushing water as you feel its caress. Feel the wind on your face. Watch the sunrise and sunset, the wildflowers in the wind, and the star-laden night sky. Feel the warmth of love down deep in your soul. Breathe in and taste the goodness of God. God made our senses and longs to inhabit each of them." Take some time to see, hear, taste, smell, and touch. On purpose. And stand in awe.

Chapter 4:
Preparing for Transition

I'm left-handed and can struggle when someone loads the dishwasher "right-handedly." I like things in the place they belong and can get frustrated when things are out of order. I confess that just today, in a public restroom in a restaurant, I "fixed" their toilet paper so it would hang the "correct" way.[22] Please don't judge me. I won't change your toilet paper, I promise. How do you do with little changes? Transitions require flexibility. Ouch.

The ways we handle the smaller things in life prepare us for the bigger ones. Bruce Feller, in his book, *Life Is in the Transitions: Mastering Change at Any Age,* notes that life is not linear and terms transitions as "lifequakes." One reviewer of his book adds to a well-known phrase as he writes, "As the saying goes 'when one door closes another one opens, but it is hell in the hallways.'" Certainly, there is a journey we must take between the doors.

Our mindset as we live each day prepares us for transitions. Whether the changes feel gut-wrenching and sudden or gradual and intentional, they rock our

---

22. According to a study conducted at the University of Colorado, the correct way to hang toilet paper is so the paper hangs over the roll, not under. (You are welcome) https://www.google.com/search?q=correct+way+to+hang+toilet+paper&rlz=1C1CHBF_enUS741US741&oq=correct+way+to+hang+tu&aqs=chrome.0.0i512j69i57j0i51212j0i22i3016.5848j0j7&sourceid=chrome&ie=UTF-8#kpvalbx=_czRgYprcLIGIptQP0sq_wAQ16.

worlds, dizzy our perspectives, numb us, overwhelm us—or make us stronger. They may threaten and destroy, or enhance and fortify our faith, depending on how we handle them; and how we handle them depends on our core convictions and beliefs. Sometimes we need to revisit those core convictions to make sure we know what they are and why we hold them.

Mary, the mother of Jesus, at a young age faced a monumental, life-changing transition. How was her faith so strong in her teen years as to not only withstand, but to victoriously maneuver through the transitions she would endure for the remainder of her life? She knew whom she had believed and was willing to let God use her. Sometimes we are better at knowing *what* we believe (which is important) than *who* we believe (which is most important).

Mary's song reveals her convictions. She *got* God's heart. She recognized God's care for her, his might, his holiness, and his mercy. She was familiar with the Scriptures as she recounted the stories from generation to generation, noting God's care for the hungry and the humble. She knew the story of Abraham and Israel. In her mind, God's promises were unwavering.

And Mary said:
"My soul glorifies the Lord
    and my spirit rejoices in God my Savior,

for he has been mindful

What Now, God?

of the humble state of his servant.
From now on all generations will call me blessed,

> *for the Mighty One has done great things for me—*
> *holy is his name.*
His mercy extends to those who fear him,
> *from generation to generation.*

He has performed mighty deeds with his arm;
> *he has scattered those who are proud in their inmost thoughts.*

He has brought down rulers from their thrones
> *but has lifted up the humble.*

He has filled the hungry with good things
> *but has sent the rich away empty.*

He has helped his servant Israel,
> *remembering to be merciful*

to Abraham and his descendants forever,
> *just as he promised our ancestors."* (Luke 1:46–55)

When we face transitions, what songs arise from within us? I am afraid I may have written different lyrics than Mary. Verse one might read, "What in the world are you thinking, God? Are you trying to destroy my life? This was nowhere in my plans. What will people think? This is a crazy idea, and I think you have the wrong person."

Nothing has helped prepare me for transitions more than devoting focused time with God to reflect, to be quiet, to "be." I know this is not easy when families are young, but any deliberate time can go a long way. During one of these focused times I purposely recounted, evaluated, expressed, and renewed my core convictions. I listened for what came to my heart, and wrote. Sometimes I just read scriptures out loud or listen to them read to me on an audio app as I try to receive from God what he is offering. I need this time and space to connect; to hear him speak to me through his Spirit, the Word, creation, and people. These times have served me well, helping to steady me through turbulent transitions.

I highly recommend taking a time to recount and renew your core values and convictions. We live from what we truly believe. I considered my faith, my emotions, my community, my theological and intellectual convictions, my vocation, my health and wellness convictions, and my stewardship; and wrote out two or three of my core values concerning each area. I wrote them based on several scriptures near to my heart and then determined to be accountable for these. I will share some of my convictions from this time, which can perhaps encourage you to think through and name your own.

Finding Core Convictions

Our lives follow our core convictions. What we believe deep in our souls determines what happens when life throws us curveballs—or hand grenades. If we don't begin with deep convictions, transitions will sweep us away like the waves crashing on our heads.

> *But when you ask, you must believe and not doubt, because the one who doubts is like a wave of the sea, blown and tossed by the wind.*
>
> *That person should not expect to receive anything from the Lord.* (James 1:6–7)

The first time I did this exercise, though there was nothing intrinsically wrong with the values I listed, I found that some centered more on *what* I believed, rather than *who* I believed. My core values centered on my actions, rather than my convictions about God. The first tempts me toward a functional response to God rather than a connecting relationship with him. What do you believe about God? This is a good starting place.

After writing these values, I took some quiet, prayerful hours at the ocean to answer some heart questions for my life. I will also include these questions. Use these practices as you wish, remembering that preparation will help you navigate transitions so they won't knock you off your feet, at least for long.

Faith core values:
- **Jesus loves me, this I know, for the Bible tells me so. My faith lies in God's indescribable love. In this love, I find my identity.**

> *Your unfailing love, O LORD, is as vast as the heavens;*

your faithfulness reaches beyond the clouds.

Your righteousness is like the mighty mountains,
your justice like the ocean depths.
You care for people and animals alike, O LORD.
How precious is your unfailing love, O God!
All humanity finds shelter
in the shadow of your wings.

You feed them from the abundance of your own house,
letting them drink from your river of delights.

For you are the fountain of life,
the light by which we see. (Psalm 36:5–9 NLT)

And so we know and rely on the love God has for us. God is love. Whoever lives in love lives in God, and God in them. (1 John 4:16)

"Teacher, which is the greatest commandment in the Law?"

Jesus replied: "'Love the Lord your God with all your heart and with all your soul and with all your mind.'

This is the first and greatest commandment.

And the second is like it: 'Love your neighbor as yourself.'

All the Law and the Prophets hang on these two commandments." (Matthew 22:36–40)

What Now, God?

- *God is faithful, and I can rest in his faithfulness.*
- **Living faith is of utmost importance to God, far surpassing any accomplishments, talents, or knowledge.**

> *Know therefore that the LORD your God is God; he is the faithful God, keeping his covenant of love to a thousand generations of those who love him and keep his commandments.* (Dueteronomy 7:9)

> *"And why do you worry about clothes? See how the flowers of the field grow. They do not labor or spin.*
> *Yet I tell you that not even Solomon in all his splendor was dressed like one of these.*
> *If that is how God clothes the grass of the field, which is here today and tomorrow is thrown into the fire, will he not much more clothe you—you of little faith?"* (Matthew 6:28–30)

> *And without faith it is impossible to please God, because anyone who comes to him must believe that he exists and that he rewards those who earnestly seek him.* (Hebrews 11:6)

> *The goal of this command is love, which comes from a pure heart and a good conscience and a sincere faith.* (1 Timothy 1:5)

Emotional core values:
- ***Jesus relates to all my emotions; as a sympathetic High Priest, he is the balm for my wounds, the safe place for my fears, the***

Preparing for Transition

forgiver of my sins, the holder of my hand.

For we do not have a high priest who is unable to empathize with our weaknesses, but we have one who has been tempted in every way, just as we are—yet he did not sin.

Let us then approach God's throne of grace with confidence, so that we may receive mercy and find grace to help us in our time of need. (Hebrews 4:15–16)

- **Emotional health stems from my thoughts, and begins with gratitude.**

  Finally, brothers and sisters, whatever is true, whatever is noble, whatever is right, whatever is pure, whatever is lovely, whatever is admirable—if anything is excellent or praiseworthy—think about such things.

  Whatever you have learned or received or heard from me, or seen in me—put it into practice. And the God of peace will be with you. (Philippians 4:8–9)

  Let the peace of Christ rule in your hearts, since as members of one body you were called to peace. And be thankful.

  Let the message of Christ dwell among you richly as you teach and admonish one another with all wisdom through psalms, hymns, and songs from the Spirit, singing to God with gratitude in your hearts. (Colossians 3:15–16)

  Above all else, guard your heart,
  for everything you do flows from it. (Proverbs 4:23)

What Now, God?

Community core values:

- ***God has put me in family. As part of God's family, I am interconnected with all my brothers and sisters. I need them, and they need me.***

> *For just as each of us has one body with many members, and these members do not all have the same function,*
>
> *so in Christ we, though many, form one body, and each member belongs to all the others.*
>
> *We have different gifts, according to the grace given to each of us. If your gift is prophesying, then prophesy in accordance with your faith;*
>
> *if it is serving, then serve; if it is teaching, then teach;*
>
> *if it is to encourage, then give encouragement; if it is giving, then give generously; if it is to lead, do it diligently; if it is to show mercy, do it cheerfully.*
>
> *Love must be sincere. Hate what is evil; cling to what is good. Be devoted to one another in love. Honor one another above yourselves.* (Romans 12:4–10)

> *"A new command I give you: Love one another. As I have loved you, so you must love one another.*
>
> *By this everyone will know that you are my disciples, if you love one another."* (John 13:34–35)

- ***The only way to family unity is humility. Jesus shows me how.***

> *Be completely humble and gentle; be patient, bearing with one another in love.*

> *Make every effort to keep the unity of the Spirit through the bond of peace.*
>
> *There is one body and one Spirit, just as you were called to one hope when you were called;*
>
> *one Lord, one faith, one baptism;*
>
> *one God and Father of all, who is over all and through all and in all.* (Ephesians 4:2–6)

> *Therefore if you have any encouragement from being united with Christ, if any comfort from his love, if any common sharing in the Spirit, if any tenderness and compassion,*
>
> *then make my joy complete by being like-minded, having the same love, being one in spirit and of one mind.*
>
> *Do nothing out of selfish ambition or vain conceit. Rather, in humility value others above yourselves,*
>
> *not looking to your own interests but each of you to the interests of the others.*
>
> *In your relationships with one another, have the same mindset as Christ Jesus.* (Philippians 2:1–5)

Theological/intellectual formation core values:
- **Learning is not for my selfish purposes, but for drawing close to Jesus and helping others do the same.**

> *You study the Scriptures diligently because you think that in them you have eternal life. These are the very Scriptures that testify about me.* (John 5:39)

What Now, God?

But in your hearts revere Christ as Lord. Always be prepared to give an answer to everyone who asks you to give the reason for the hope that you have. But do this with gentleness and respect,

keeping a clear conscience, so that those who speak maliciously against your good behavior in Christ may be ashamed of their slander. (1 Peter 3:15–16)

- **God is not impressed with my knowledge, but rather with love and humility as a self-aware learner.**

    The Sovereign LORD has given me a well-instructed tongue,
    > *to know the word that sustains the weary.*
    He wakens me morning by morning,
    > *wakens my ear to listen like one being instructed.*
    (Isaiah 50:4)

    Now about food sacrificed to idols: We know that "We all possess knowledge." But knowledge puffs up while love builds up.

    Those who think they know something do not yet know as they ought to know.

    But whoever loves God is known by God. (1 Corinthians 8:1–3)

- ***I will be a continual learner.***

    "Come to me, all you who are weary and burdened,

and I will give you rest.

Take my yoke upon you and learn from me, for I am gentle and humble in heart, and you will find rest for your souls. (Matthew 11:28-29)

Vocational formation core values:

- ***Whatever my occupation, my preoccupation is the kingdom of God.***

    But seek first his kingdom and his righteousness, and all these things will be given to you as well. (Matthew 6:33)

    Then he said to them all: "If anyone would come after me, he must deny himself and take up his cross daily and follow me.

    For whoever wants to save his life will lose it, but whoever loses his life for me will save it.

    What good is it for a man to gain the whole world, and yet lose or forfeit his very self?" (Luke 9:23–25)

- ***My job does not define my identity, but my identity (in Christ) defines the ways I function within a job.***

    Whatever you do, work at it with all your heart, as working for the Lord, not for human masters,

    since you know that you will receive an inheritance from the Lord as a reward. It is the Lord Christ you are serving. (Colossians 3:23–24)

What Now, God?

Physical health and wellness core values:

- ***God makes his home in me, and thus my physical body should be a welcoming and well-kept environment. This includes nutrition, exercise, renewal, stress reduction, sleep, and purity.***

> *Don't you realize that your body is the temple of the Holy Spirit, who lives in you and was given to you by God? You do not belong to yourself, for God bought you with a high price. So you must honor God with your body.* (1 Corinthians 6:19–20 NLT)

> *Have nothing to do with irreverent, silly myths. Rather train yourself for godliness; for while bodily training is of some value, godliness is of value in every way, as it holds promise for the present life and also for the life to come.* (1 Timothy 4:7–8 ESV)

- ***God is big enough to carry my burdens.***

> *For a child has been born—for us!*
>   *the gift of a son—for us!*
> *He'll take over*
>   *the running of the world.*
> *His names will be: Amazing Counselor,*
>   *Strong God,*
> *Eternal Father,*
>   *Prince of Wholeness.*

His ruling authority will grow,
  and there'll be no limits to the wholeness he brings.
He'll rule from the historic David throne
  over that promised kingdom.
He'll put that kingdom on a firm footing
  and keep it going
With fair dealing and right living,
  beginning now and lasting always.
The zeal of GOD-of-the-Angel-Armies
  will do all this. (Isaiah 9:6–7 MSG)

"And I will ask the Father, and he will give you another advocate to help you and be with you forever—

the Spirit of truth. The world cannot accept him, because it neither sees him nor knows him. But you know him, for he lives with you and will be in you.

I will not leave you as orphans; I will come to you." (John 14:16–18)

Resource/stewardship core values:
- **Generosity reflects the heart of God and requires both my planning and spontaneity.**

Surely the righteous will never be shaken;
  they will be remembered forever.

They will have no fear of bad news;
  their hearts are steadfast, trusting in the LORD.
Their hearts are secure, they will have no fear;
  in the end they will look in triumph on their foes.

What Now, God?

They have freely scattered their gifts to the poor,
their righteousness endures forever;
their horn will be lifted high in honor. (Psalm 112:6–9)

Remember this: Whoever sows sparingly will also reap sparingly, and whoever sows generously will also reap generously.

Each of you should give what you have decided in your heart to give, not reluctantly or under compulsion, for God loves a cheerful giver.

And God is able to bless you abundantly, so that in all things at all times, having all that you need, you will abound in every good work.

As it is written:

"They have freely scattered their gifts to the poor;
their righteousness endures forever."

Now he who supplies seed to the sower and bread for food will also supply and increase your store of seed and will enlarge the harvest of your righteousness.

You will be enriched in every way so that you can be generous on every occasion, and through us your generosity will result in thanksgiving to God. (2 Corinthians 9:6–11)

"You should tithe, yes, but do not neglect the more important things." (Luke 11:42b NLT)

"It is more blessed to give than to receive." (Acts 20:35)

"Give, and it will be given to you. A good measure, pressed down, shaken together and running over, will be *poured into your lap. For with the measure you use, it will be measured to you."* (Luke 6:38)

- **God has gifted me with gifts unique to me. I will use them to benefit others and continually grow in them.**

    Christ himself gave the apostles, the prophets, the evangelists, the pastors and teachers,
    to equip his people for works of service, so that the body of Christ may be built up
    until we all reach unity in the faith and in the knowledge of the Son of God and become mature, attaining to the whole measure of the fullness of Christ. (Ephesians 4:11–13)

    In Christ we, though many, form one body, and each member belongs to all the others.
    We have different gifts, according to the grace given to each of us. If your gift is prophesying, then prophesy in accordance with your faith; if it is serving, then serve; if it is teaching, then teach; if it is to encourage, then give encouragement; if it is giving, then give generously; if it is to lead, do it diligently; if it is to show mercy, do it cheerfully. (Romans 12:5–8)

(Note: I used Clifton's Strength finder, the Enneagram, and *Discover Your God-Given Gifts* by Don and Katie Fortune as resources to help me assess my strengths and weaknesses.)

What Now, God?

A Personal Retreat

When I take time away, I do different things. Sometimes these times are planned, and sometimes I just sit or walk with God. Here is a sample of some questions I have used during such a time. The following were questions given to me for a class assignment.

Personal Retreat Reflection Questions

- What have you discovered or has been confirmed about your unique design and calling (for example, strengths, talents/abilities/skills, personality, and spiritual giftings)? Take time to list them. Then offer yourself anew to God through a written prayer of surrender.

- When was the last time you experienced the Lord's love for you personally? Describe this time. If none comes to mind, ask him to reveal his love for you now in a tangible way. Close with a prayer to God acknowledging his love for you, asking him to reveal more of his love to you, and expressing your love to him.

- What lingering relational conflicts might be unresolved that you would like to ask the Lord to pour his grace upon in order to release and heal you and another/others to move forward unhindered in his purposes? Is there anything that he would want you to acknowledge, confess, and/or do to mend the situation? Include a written prayer to God related to this.

- Are there any circumstances or personal issues hindering you from being completely available to the Lord to fulfill your calling?

- When was the last time you enjoyed something you really like to do (e.g. recreational, something fun)? Briefly describe this time, then describe how you can add more life-giving activity to your life over the next few months.

- What has been your greatest disappointment over the last few years?

- As you look to the future, what is your greatest fear?

- As you look to the future, what is your greatest hope?

When navigating transitions, whether or not you find such exercises helpful, core convictions tether us to a raft that gives us confidence and hope when transition waves come crashing. Our convictions may roll along with us, but they anchor us. No matter the transitions, we can stand firm, holding on to the only hand that is able to keep us from falling.

> *If I rise on the wings of the dawn,*
> *if I settle on the far side of the sea,*
> *even there your hand will guide me,*
> *your right hand will hold me fast.* (Psalm 139:9–10)

What Now, God?

Time Is Filled with Swift Transition
By Chris Condon
Acworth, Georgia

Transitions are uncomfortable. Change upsets a delicate balance set in place. My family experienced transition after transition, and thus raising the family was much like the balancing game of Jenga, where pulling the odd loose piece out from under was not as difficult as adding it carefully back on top. We are a blended family. Our trust in each other was not built with natural or conventional progression, and every change brought new challenges with trust issues. At times, we required a third party to help us work things out. Often, we needed to stop and ask God to somehow intervene. My children were at times open to the idea of prayer, as it gave them an opportunity to air their concerns, fears, petitions, and anger without correction or lecture from me, the stepfather. It also gave them an opportunity to hear me ask God for his wisdom, his revelation and will, not my own. I often felt like a failure as I found myself on unstable and unrecognizable ground as a young parent of teens and preteens. I felt as though I had no business being in such a position and that these children deserved better.

When I married my wife, I received an immediate family. We learned to laugh together, and during much of the early times I had them laughing at me. Humility is powerful. I didn't understand many concepts God was teaching me about trust at the time, but I trusted that what he teaches us is true.

Jesus said, "Blessed are the pure in heart, for they shall see God." As a young man, these words did not feel tangible for my current, real life. Without needed understanding, I found his words nearly impossible to live up to, and over time I became frustrated.

Preparing for Transition

But I grew.

Over time, through the love, grace, and patience of God, my wife, my family, and my church I learned that with a pure heart, I could see God all around me. And I did. Some might say that I wore rose-colored glasses, as the world around me is dirty, callous, and corrupt. They aren't wrong about that, though the existence of evil doesn't minimize the presence of God. I saw this clearly in God's creation, in people, and especially in my wife's transition story, which also became mine.

Early in 2019, when my wife MaryBeth was fifty-seven years old, she learned that she had been adopted as a newborn. She had previously thought she was an Italian girl from Boston and Somerville, Massachusetts. When MaryBeth was born, she had not been expected to live beyond a few days. She had serious birth defects. Her birth mother gave her up in a backdoor adoption. Her adoptive parents couldn't have children, and since the state decided they were not fit to adopt, the birth mother conducted the adoption "underground," without the state.

MaryBeth's adoptive mother spent most of two years taking care of MaryBeth in the hospital, before and after major surgeries. Recently, MaryBeth found out that her now-deceased birth father was a well-known person in New England, a professor of music, conductor, and musical accompanist on a well-known television program. As far as she knew, her father had no knowledge of her existence. Even if he had known, he was married to a woman other than her birth mother. He had two children with his wife, and the knowledge of MaryBeth would probably have been so embarrassing that her birth defects would have been a convenient solution to end her life. She would likely never have gotten the support to make it beyond a few days.

MaryBeth grew up in an alcoholic environment. She was beaten and mistreated as a young child and as a teenager, rescued from time to time by her aunt. She was placed in foster care due to the amount of abuse in the home. The same people who worked so hard for her survival in infancy and adolescence threatened her life many times during alcoholic-induced rage.

In her first marriage, MaryBeth endured a husband who was not trustworthy and was violent. Throughout her experience with this man, God protected her. MaryBeth became a follower of Jesus and decided to trust in him. We met and married several years later. It was clear to me that I married a woman who was a daughter of God. It was clear that God cared for my wife even through such challenging times. Her transition from a lack of trust in unreliable earthly fathers to her trust in a loving heavenly Father changed her life, and mine. This transition prepared her for all others.

Fast forward to January 2020. COVID-19 arrived. My wife of twenty-four years had significant health issues, and her doctors told her to stay home. She stayed home with limited outside visits. Between the political craziness, yearlong disruptions of civility in major cities, and this virus, hope seemed to diminish. During this time MaryBeth doubled down on her commitment to prayer and study of God's word. She made sure she reached out to anyone who crossed her mind, as she was convinced it was God's Spirit encouraging her to make the connections. MaryBeth could not escape COVID's reach, was hospitalized, and on December 3, transitioned to the other side of eternity.

Her transition from this life to the next was preceded with love, appreciation, and concern for everyone around her. She had asked us all to pray for her nurses, doctors, technicians, and dietary staff. She was in the caring hands of the Father she had learned to trust even though her earthly fathers failed her. It was always her heavenly Father who paid her passage, who fed and clothed her. It was God who stayed with her on the side of the road and in the face of grave danger from those she should have been able to trust. God held her close to him, especially when things seemed desperate. And now he holds her closer still.

> Time is filled with swift transition,
> Naught of earth unmoved can stand,
> Build your hopes on things eternal,
> Hold to God's unchanging hand.
>
> Trust in him who will not leave you,
> Whatsoever years may bring,
> If by earthly friends forsaken
> Still more closely to him cling.
>
> When your journey is completed,
> If to God you have been true,
> Fair and bright the home in glory
> Your enraptured soul will view.

(Hymn by Jennie Wilson, 1906)

What Now, God?

Reflections on Transition Preparation

Our ability to find God amid our transitions depends on our core convictions about God. We can easily assume core convictions without really naming them or thinking them through. Without holding deep core convictions, we can be easily swept off our feet when transitions come. Reflect and recount your core convictions in each of the areas listed. Consider what your convictions really are, not what you think they should be. Accompany your convictions with scripture and determine ways you can intentionally grow in these convictions.

My faith core values: _____

My emotional core values: _____

My community core values: _____

My theological/intellectual core values: _____

My vocational core values: _____

My health/wellness core values: _____

My resource/stewardship core values: _____

Consider taking a spiritual retreat and reflecting on questions such as:

- What have you discovered or has been confirmed about your unique design and calling (for example, strengths, talents/abilities/skills, personality, and spiritual giftings)? Take time to list them. Then offer yourself anew to God through a written prayer of surrender.

- When was the last time you experienced the Lord's love for you personally? Describe this time. If none comes to mind, ask him to reveal his love for you now in a tangible way. Close with a prayer to God acknowledging his love for you, asking him to reveal more of his love to you, and expressing your love to him.

- What lingering relational conflicts might be unresolved that you would like to ask the Lord to pour his grace upon in order to release and heal you and another to move forward unhindered in his purposes? Is there anything that he would want you to acknowledge, confess, and/or do to mend the situation? Include a written prayer to God related to this.

- Are there any circumstances or personal issues hindering you from being completely available to the Lord to fulfill your calling?

- When was the last time you enjoyed something you really like to do (i.e., recreational, creative, something fun)? Briefly describe this time, then explore how you can add more life-giving activity to your life over the next few months.

- What has been your greatest disappointment over the last few years?

- As you look to the future, what is your greatest fear?

- As you look to the future, what is your greatest hope?

Chapter 5:
Raise Your Ebenezer—
Marking Transitions

I note in the Bible how often transitions, big and small, were commemorated. Stones of remembrance were stacked. Feasts were held. Garments were torn. Bread was broken. Altars were built. I find it helpful to mark transitions rather than just letting them slide by. It helps me, although I realize that people have different ways of processing transitions. This is not a one-size-fits-all thought process.

For most of my life, I have assumed that icons and liturgy were detractors from the true message of Jesus and substitutes for closeness to God. Lately, I have thought differently as I continually seek to build connection more closely with him. Yes, forms and traditions can replace relationship, but forms and traditions can also enhance relationships when the heart stays engaged. The Bible is full of liturgy and symbols. These were important parts of life in ancient Judaism and the Middle Eastern world. We miss a richer dimension of meaning in Jesus' teachings and parables when we are unfamiliar with ancient Middle Eastern feasts, symbols, festivals, and practices. For example, John 7:37–38 tells us:

What Now, God?

> *On the last and greatest day of the festival, Jesus stood and said in a loud voice, "Let anyone who is thirsty come to me and drink.*
>
> *Whoever believes in me, as Scripture has said, rivers of living water will flow from within them."*

Jesus' declaration of himself as living water takes on greater meaning when we understand what was happening during the last and greatest day of this festival. This Festival of the Tabernacles, or Sukkot, commemorates the forty years the Israelites spent in the desert on the way to the promised land. Many historians believe that on this last day of the festival, the water libation ceremony (the pouring of water) reached its climax. Presumedly, the priests circled the altar seven times and with grandeur and ceremony, poured out water. This was Hoshana Rabbah, or "HOSHIANA," which is translated "save now." This was an appeal to the Creator God to provide water for the people.[23]

Can you imagine the impact of this moment when Jesus suddenly declares in a loud voice, "Let anyone who is thirsty, come to me and drink?" I get chills thinking about this.

Rites of Passage

Many non-American cultures practice celebrations of passage into different life stages. A Dutch Anthro-

---

23. https://jewsforjesus.org/publications/issues/issues-v06-n07/sukkot-a-promise-of-living-water/.

pologist, Arnold van Gennep, interpreted these rites for Western cultures and coined the term "rites of passage." These were the "ways in which traditional societies structured life transitions."[24] Author William Bridges describes van Gennep's work:

> He grouped together rituals dealing with birth and death, puberty and marriage; with the election of a chief and the creation of a shaman; with an individual's entry into a secret society of men or women and with nature's passage into a new season. He also saw that these ceremonial occasions consisted of three phases, which he called separation, transition, and incorporation.[25]

Bridges renames these Endings, The Neutral Zone, and The New Beginning.[26] These markings also coincide with Bruggeman's structure of the Psalms into Orientation, Disorientation, and Reorientation. Bridges, in studying these customs, notes that the "rituals of passage are simply a way of focusing and making more visible the natural patterns of dying, chaos, and renewal that was believed to operate everywhere in the universe. And without that belief, there is nothing to focus."[27]

Commemorating can bring us back to God's heart. Commemorations remind us of his love and provision

---

24. William Bridges, *Transitions: Making Sense of Life's Changes* (Cambridge, MA: Da Capo Press, 2004), 103.
25. Bridges, *Transitions*, 104.
26. Bridges, *Transitions*, 104.
27. Bridges, *Transitions*, 104.

and make space for our gratitude. God had reasons for implementing commemorative celebrations, whether it was celebrating safe passage through lands, parting seas, finding wells, victories over enemies, care through floods and famines, the saving of Israel's firstborn, or dedication or rededication of temples. Stones of remembrance were placed one on top of the other, sacrifices were made, incense was burned, feasts were had, candles were lit, prayers were prayed, and ebenezers were raised. These all were tangible, participatory celebrations, rituals, liturgies, and remembrances meant to bring to mind God's love, bring his people together, and bring all to gratitude.

Sensory, tangible expressions marking transitions move connections deeper into our souls and serve as reminders of God's presence. When God met Moses on Mount Sinai, he sent him back not only with tablets of commandments, but also a recipe for oil. Rachel Held Evans explains that this oil would anoint the temple, altar, temple furnishings, and even the priests. It was reserved for these special, sacred places. No one else was to use it (Exodus 30:22–28). God knew what we now know, that the olfactory nerve is connected to the amygdala, the part of the brain associated with memory and emotion. Certain smells can flood our memory. God wanted people to know his scent, to remember.[28]

Nearly two hundred biblical references speak of oil to light lamps, to sooth dry skin, to honor guests, to mark

---

28. Rachel Held Evans, *Searching for Sunday* (Nashville, TN: Thomas Nelson, 2015), 203.

a sacred place, to entice, to comfort, consecrate, heal, anoint, or prepare a body for burial. To the ancient Israelites, prayer smelled like frankincense. This was said to be sweet to God's senses.[29] How cool is it that God has senses! We are created in the image of God, and our communication and connection to him brings pleasing aroma. Held continues, "There is nothing magic about oil. It is merely a carrier—of memory, of healing, of grace. We anoint not to cure, but to heal. We anoint to soothe, to dignify, and even in our suffering, to remember the scent of God."[30]

Raise Your Ebenezer

So, what is an ebenezer and why should we raise one? This word was in a beautiful hymn ("O Thou Fount of Every Blessing") that I often heard as a child, but I didn't understand its meaning. Every time we got to that word in the song, I found the eyes of another kid in the church, and we chuckled at the strange word. But it's a good word. After a God-given victory over the Philistines, Samuel "took a stone and set it up between Mizpah and Shen. He named it Ebenezer, saying, 'Thus far has the Lord helped us.'

So the Philistines were subdued and did not invade Israelite territory again. Throughout Samuel's lifetime, the hand of the Lord was against the Philistines" (1 Samuel 7:12–13). The Ebenezer was a stone reminding

---

29. Evans, *Searching for Sunday*, 204.
30. Evans, *Searching for Sunday*, 205.

the Israelites of God's help.

Ancient Jewish festivals were linked with seasons in nature. Passover, originally a spring festival, became a celebration of the exodus from Egypt. The Feast of Weeks, a festival at the end of the wheat harvest (Exodus 23:16; 34:22), became a celebration for the day the Torah was given at Sinai. The Feast of Booths, an old vintage festival, commemorates the Israelites dwelling in booths during their wilderness journey (Leviticus 23:42). To Israel, the unique events of history were more important spiritually than the long-celebrated repeat cycles of nature.[31]

These icons, remembrances, and feasts, such as the Lord's Supper we commemorate today, all help to remind us of God's loving presence and mighty deeds. God loves a party. When we remember his love given to us and his presence within us, we renew or strengthen our focus on his identity and on our identity as his image bearers.

But It Feels Weird

Are you scared of icons and remembrances like I was? Do they feel weird? I would say, "Try it. You may like it." This past year, during what is commonly known as the season of Lent, I practiced a series of fasts laid out in a book called *40 Days of Decrease*. This was a highlight in my year and something I plan to repeat. I have collected and stacked stones of remembrance and

---

31. Abraham Joshua Heschel, *The Sabbath* (NY: Macmillan, 1951), 7.

I may have even lit some candles during Advent to help my heart more deeply commemorate and celebrate the coming and birth of Christ. This did my heart good, and my holiday was richer because of it.

This summer I meditated as I walked a labyrinth, and last week I conducted a *Lectio Divina* exercise for several hundred Christians in our church. Their overwhelming response was that it deeply fed their souls. I was not surprised, because these practices help make space for the Word to be alive in our lives, to do its work. This allows the Spirit to direct us as we listen more carefully to God. These are simply tools that help me center my heart and actions on God, reminding me to not just *do,* but to *connect* more deeply with God. These practices are centuries old, yet we can let our fear of falling into tradition keep us from experiencing meaningful Christian practices.

For people like me, who like things neat, tidy, certain, rational, and predictable, it is easy to resist letting go of our control over all things godly. These new additions to my life are meant to enhance my walk with God, allowing me to experience him more fully with all my senses. I firmly believe that a deeper relationship with God results in a brighter reflection of his image toward those with whom we interact, including those with whom we might not naturally interact without the urging of God that we gain from these contemplative times. I, for one, need to raise my ebenezers more often. In doing this, I allow God free rein to engage my God-given senses in a greater experience of him. This has brought great refreshment and rest to my soul.

Marking Transitions

After losing my husband, I desperately longed to hear his voice again, to feel his warm hug, to smell his stinky fish-handling hands, to feel my hand in his, to touch his face and hair, to witness his victories and defeats and have him do the same for me. No surprise that yesterday, when putting away Christmas decorations, I found an ugly, blue foam foot pad that had helped protect Wyndham's heel from bedsores. I had kept it on purpose. With tears, I smothered my face in the foam pad and breathed in, hoping to steal just one more memory, one more connection, one more touch. Wyndham's foot protector became an ebenezer.

I can no longer experience the physical embrace, and I think this has resulted in my deepening hunger to feel the touch of God more closely. For this, I am grateful. I don't plan to quit this search anytime soon.

Consider ways you might more deliberately conduct "ending and beginning" celebrations for moves, job changes, and all kinds of transitions. On the last night before the house I had lived in for over thirty years was sold, I gathered my kids and grandkids together. Since there was no furniture, we had pizza on the floor and recounted our favorite memories in the home. I treasure that time and am very grateful we did that. I think it is important to celebrate birthdays, even if a celebration can only be done virtually. In our family birthday celebrations, we follow a custom of "one-word encouragements" (with modifying sentences following) for the birthday person. These are needed and special for both kids and adults. Celebrate whatever you can, and mourn or mark the exiting transitions as well. These commemorations help us move through transitions with remembrance, mourning, gratitude, and closure. The "pictures" we paint in these times form deeper sinews into our hearts that stay with us for the future. In marking transitions, we can better get in touch with endings, neutral zones, and new beginnings; separation, transition, and incorporation; and orientation, disorientation, and reorientation. In other words, they help us move through transitions. John Eldridge pens this need in his book, *Get Your Life Back,* "I believe in rituals; they are the last signposts left in a culture of impermanence."[32]

Turning the Tide

I *choose* to count my blessings. And I name them. This has become a passion and habit for me. Negativity, even from trauma and pain, quickly gains momentum, digs deeper holes, and becomes self-propagating when we let our thoughts sit too long in it. I have found that recounting the blessings and joys of life must become intentional, a spiritual discipline. Commemorating our blessings through various means such as physical remembrances, writings, pictures, poems, or pizza on the

---

32. John Eldridge, *Get Your Life Back*, 57.

floor is a sacramental move toward the curl of the wave, helping us resist the opposing tides of darkness and loss.

As the one-year anniversary of my husband's death approached, I wondered how the day would feel. Would I celebrate his one-year heavenly birthday, mourn his loss, look at pictures, relive the horrible day, all of the above, or something else altogether? While we commemorate certain holidays, many life transitions (both the encouraging and the oh-so-hard ones) pass by us unmarked. Not commemorated. Unconfronted. I believe this can make transitions more difficult to pass through, leaving us emotionally stuck. I knew I did not want to simply dread this one-year anniversary, so in preparation, I talked with God about what might be most helpful. Perhaps the Spirit put some thoughts in my head, but by whatever means they arrived, they were helpful. The day was deeply meaningful and special.

I considered that as an entire family it might help us to mark the day together. So on that day, we each took several hours to get away. We went out in nature, Wyndham's favorite place to be on this side of heaven. God blessed the day with unseasonably warm, gorgeous weather. One of us went to a riverside, another to the cleft in a rock at the reservoir, and several others to the ocean. I went to our special beach in Manchester-by-the-Sea, a place where we had spent many Mondays walking, praying, talking, dreaming, and planning. It felt more inspiring than sad to be there. As I felt the sun warming my face and the waves gently sliding over the sand, I sang, listened to spiritual music, read, journaled, prayed, and listened to learn. We all began our times with an intent to still our hearts—to breathe in as we invited the Spirit to fill our hearts and breathe out the distractions and anxieties. As we each "retreated," we reflected on and journaled some of the following questions:

- What do you most remember Papa saying to you that you carry with you? What do you think he would most want to say to you today?
- What do you think God would want to say to you today?
- What is at least one way that this very hard year has helped you grow spiritually?
- What is a scripture or song that has helped sustain you this past year?
- What are your best memories from this year?
- What are you most grateful to God for as you think through his work in your life this year?
- What are a few of your favorite thoughts/hopes about heaven?

This was a profound, helpful ebenezer exercise for me, and for each of us. We also commemorated November 21 as our first annual "Pay It Forward for Papa Day." We each decided on some special good deeds to do in honor of him. This was fun, meaningful, and fitting.

Reflections

We ended the night with a several-hour Zoom call in which we each shared our special moments from the day. It was honest, vulnerable, full of laughter, and full of tears. I treasure that time.

I also took a few pictures of my time at the beach. I captured a father and child frolicking hand in hand, sharing pure joy. I felt grateful to have a heavenly Father who takes my hand. I accompanied this view, singing the song: "Precious Lord, take my hand, lead me on, let me stand... Through the storms, through the night, lead me on to the light... Take my hand, precious Lord, lead me home."

Next, I watched kayakers set out across the sparkling water toward a destination I couldn't see. This scene reminded me of my new journey, one in which I must trust God because I don't know exactly where my path will take me. After the kayakers, I saw a young couple walk toward the water and ever so calmly and gently glide their swimsuit-clad bodies into the ocean without even a second's hesitation. They walked in as if the ocean was bathwater and then floated neck-deep in the 51-degree water. (Yes, I googled the temperature.) After about ten minutes of their stillness in the water, I lost track of my prayers and tried to remember my college life-saving class drills in case I would be needed to retrieve hypothermic floaters. Fortunately, they calmly and slowly walked back to shore and dabbed themselves with towels.

As I watched them walk into the frigid water without hesitation, I thought of the song "Oceans," and the lyrics spoke to me. Could I walk out into uncomfortable waters as calmly as that, or would I be wailing and screaming with the discomfort? I sang some words to the song: "You call me out upon the waters, the great unknown where feet may fail."

God guides us to the curl of the wave. Though I felt I had experienced an inexpressibly difficult year of transitions, perhaps it was the year when I grew the most. One step at a time.

Beware of Boredom-Induced Transitions

Sometimes we choose transitions. Be careful of choosing transitions because you are bored with sameness. We can become restless souls at times, especially when things get tough. Do you find yourself wanting change when facing difficulties, whether in a job, in a relationship, or when you are "stuck" in your own character weaknesses? Sometimes it feels easier to move on than to persevere through tough situations. While at times external changes are helpful, often the needed changes come from within. If you often feel that the grass will be greener on the other side of the fence, remember that you take you with you wherever you go.

Through prayer, the Bible, and wise spiritual counsel, determine whether the transitions you choose are truly for God's purposes, or if they are self-seeking. Will the transition you are considering:

- Help you be more faithful to God?
- Bring more godly peace in your life?
- Encourage you and your family to grow stronger spiritually?
- Enable you to be more involved in the family of God?
- Allow you to be more connected to God and others, thereby more effective in reaching this lost world?

The best transition we can make, no matter the circumstance or geography involved, is the transition from one degree of glory to another. If a physical or experiential transition isn't feasible or best, we can always transition our thinking. That's the best kind of transition.

> *And we, who with unveiled faces all reflect the Lord's glory, are being transformed into his likeness with ever-increasing glory, which comes from the Lord, who is the Spirit.* (2 Corinthians 3:18)

When we determine to grow through our transitions, the situations in which we find ourselves will be the ones where God can best use us. Then, as our hearts grow closer to God, the grass under our feet suddenly becomes greener.

Whatever your transition, God is strong enough to carry you through it. You may feel like you are spinning and being spit out in the ocean, but God will help you find the curl in the wave. He is the curl in the wave. Your boundaries can become pleasant ones, as there is always beauty to see and something for which we can be grateful, depending on our perspective. God can use our transitions to his glory, no matter what they are. Pray to embrace your transitions, pleasant or difficult. Let God counsel and instruct you so that even when you are tossed about, you will not be shaken.

> *LORD, you have assigned me my portion and my cup;*
> *you have made my lot secure.*
>
> *The boundary lines have fallen for me in pleasant places;*
> *surely I have a delightful inheritance.*
>
> *I will praise the LORD, who counsels me;*
> *even at night my heart instructs me.*
>
> *I have set the LORD always before me.*
> *Because he is at my right hand,*
> *I will not be shaken.* (Psalms 16:5–8 NIV1984)

And we know that in all things God works for the good of those who love him, who have been called according to his purpose. (Romans 8:28)

What Now, God?

Transformation in Transition
By Alexandra Ghoman
Charleston, South Carolina

I've been thinking about New England autumns. The transformation that can seemingly happen overnight—one day it's a hot Boston summer and the next, the air is crisp and smells like crunchy leaves and postseason baseball. It's change. And it can sneak up on you.

But this year, we've traded in our boots for flipflops and our apple picking for oyster roasts. Uprooting is such an adventure. It's beautiful and fun and full but also refining and lonely and eye-opening.

Mostly, I feel thankful. Many people live their whole lives in one place, and while I imagine that yields a special kind of continuity and security (would love to know more about that life), here I am, collecting memories, friendships, and knowledge from this crazy thing we call change.

And we all know how change is. Change is good. But even the best of changes is challenging. Isn't it funny how you see yourself differently in a different place or circumstance? Maybe it's not a new place, but a new stage, relationship, or job. Your weaknesses stick out a little more and your strengths look a little different. You find pieces of yourself exposed that were comfortably hidden away before. And those pieces are now nudged toward growth, stretched toward progress, and bent toward…well, change.

But even as I feel these nudges and pushes, I'm trying to remember that it's part of the sanctification process. And what is sanctification? Just a fancy word for being made holy. Being made (ahem…nudged, pushed, discipled) into the person God created me to be. So even though I feel like squishing those jagged edges back into places of comfort and ease, it's okay. I can lean into the exposure, trusting that something beautiful is happening here.

The leaves may not be changing to triumphant New England colors for me this season, but I hope I am. And I guess that's pretty beautiful too.

> *Don't copy the behavior and customs of this world, but let God transform you into a new person by changing the way you think. Then you will learn to know God's will for you, which is good and pleasing and perfect.* (Romans 12:2 NLT)

What Now, God?

Reflections on Ebenezers

What are some transitions that you have marked, and how did you do so? What did you learn from these times?

The Bible recounts many visible, tangible types of "ebenezers" in the Bible. Consider ways you might more deliberately conduct "ending and beginning" celebrations for moves, job changes, losses, celebrations, and all kinds of transitions. What are some ways you might initiate marking transitions in your own life or helping others mark theirs? Consider choosing one to implement within the next few months.

At the end of each day, practice recounting blessings from God you experienced that day. Name several.

Consider new transitions you may be considering. Ask yourself. Will this transition:

- Help me be more faithful to God?
- Bring more godly peace in my life?
- Encourage me and my family to grow stronger spiritually?
- Enable me to be more involved in the family of God?
- Allow me to be more connected to God and others, thereby more joined with God's mission for my life?

Chapter 6: Transitions That Overflow

Transitions change us. They transform us. Think of your most recent major transition. How did you feel while going through it? If you are still in a time of transition, do you find yourself feeling emptier and more confused, thrashing in the waves...or do you feel solid ground under your feet, even if you haven't found the exact curl of the wave? It may be hard to imagine any feelings of exhilaration, or even the satisfaction of riding the wave.

Transitions take things from us, often leaving us with an empty, hollow feeling in our gut. The hollowness seems to grow deeper; but for real, it can be filled. I am convinced that "finding God" in our everyday lives is the only way to stop the drainage and fill our souls. Jeremiah prophesies to a transitioning, hurting, draining Israel:

> Lord, you are the hope of Israel;
> > all who forsake you will be put to shame.
> Those who turn away from you will be written in the dust
> > because they have forsaken the LORD,
> > **the spring of living water.**
> **Heal me,** LORD, and I will be healed;
> > save me and I will be saved,
> > for you are the one I praise.
> (Jeremiah 17:13–14, emphasis added)

When We Feel Empty

We can easily relate to the parts of the above scripture that speak of shame or turning away. We can imagine our names written in the dust, though we long to read our names through the spray from springs of living water. *Healing* and *saving* may feel out of reach for us—perhaps because they are. It is when we realize we don't have it all together that we become more open to receiving rather than pretending we have all we need within us. I don't know about you, but I have a hard time receiving. I much prefer to be on the giving end, lest I feel "needy." So, if I feel emptiness gnawing within, I give more and work harder. This works for a while, but only for a while. My house is never cleaner than when I am going through a difficult transition. I suppose I think that busyness will make the hurt disappear or that I will feel more worthwhile with production. Some people respond this way, while others feel unable to accomplish much of anything. Both are ways of managing grief.

The Apostle John, in John 4, records a time when Jesus approached a Samaritan woman with the offer of a gift. An outcast, she had little to offer except a cup of physical water. Jesus exchanged her meager cup, along with her brokenness and vulnerability, for living water.

> Jesus answered her, "If you knew the gift of God and who it is that asks you for a drink, you would have asked him and he would have given you **living water**." (John 4:10, emphasis added)

Remember, this was also Jesus' bold acclamation at the conclusion of the Festival of the Temples in John 7:37–39:

> *"Let anyone who is thirsty come to me and drink. Whoever believes in me, as Scripture has said, rivers of living water will flow from within them."*
>
> By this he meant the Spirit, *whom those who believed in him were later to receive. Up to that time the Spirit had not been given, since Jesus had not yet been glorified"* (emphasis mine).

What does it mean to drink from the stream of living water flowing within—to drink from the Spirit? Do we miss the fact that this living water, the Spirit, is a gift? This. Is. A. Gift. A gift we must receive. Though we receive the Spirit's indwelling at rebirth (John 3:5–8; Ac 2:38), it isn't a one-and-done reception. The Spirit continually fills, refreshes, counsels, comforts, leads, guides, and confirms. As author David Takle explains:

> "The Holy Spirit is not someone who follows us around and gives us a booster shot when we try to do good things. He is the one that we are supposed to follow! He is the active leader, and we are to learn to live by his direction... He was given to us as a life-giving companion and mentor with whom we would have direct contact."[33]

---

33. David Takle, *Forming: A Work of Grace* (High Point, NC: Kingdom Formation Ministries, 2013), 28.

When we receive this living water, we drink from God himself, God in us, engaging with him in ways that change our hearts.

Learning to Receive

It is hard to read the Bible to receive. *Really* receive. It is easier to take away a list of to-do's or should-have-done, but this leaves us burdened rather than refreshed. When I quickly gravitate to the things I need to do, I am reading backward. If I allow the Spirit to fill me with "rivers of living water," then the things I *do* spring from *who I am becoming* from the inside out. Let's take a moment to try receiving from the Spirit. Read these verses from Jesus, describing his life-giving gifts to us. Try reading them out loud, several times. Reading the Scriptures aloud, repetitively, often brings new insights. Read to receive. Take it all in as you read the following:

> *Then Jesus declared, "I am the bread of life. Whoever comes to me will never go hungry, and whoever believes in me will never be thirsty."* (John 6:35)

> *When Jesus spoke again to the people, he said, "I am the light of the world. Whoever follows me will never walk in darkness, but will have the light of life."* (John 8:12)

> *"I am the good shepherd. The good shepherd lays down his life for the sheep...*

> "I am the good shepherd; I know my sheep and my sheep know me—
>
> just as the Father knows me and I know the Father—and I lay down my life for the sheep." (John 10:11, 14–15)

> "I will not leave you as orphans; I will come to you.
>
> Before long, the world will not see me anymore, but you will see me. Because I live, you also will live. On that day you will realize that I am in my Father, and you are in me, and I am in you...
>
> But the Advocate, the Holy Spirit, whom the Father will send in my name, will teach you all things and will remind you of everything I have said to you.
>
> Peace I leave with you; my peace I give you. I do not give to you as the world gives. Do not let your hearts be troubled and do not be afraid." (John 14:18–20, 26–27)

Can you feel the difference between reading for knowledge, reading for practice, and reading to be filled by God? All are needed, but I believe we often neglect the latter.

When we experience God, when we *find* him as we go through transitions, he not only fills the empty, gaping wounds in our soul, but he can fill them to overflowing. This sounds too good to be true. How can someone going through all kinds of transitions, especially painful ones, have anything left to give? And even if by sheer determination we manage to eke out something that resembles giving, "overflowing" would not be the word choice to describe the condition of our heart.

But something amazing happens when we begin to grasp the enormity of God. When we allow ourselves to *receive* that living water and take in the bread that fills us, contentment follows. This is more than a theological understanding. Receiving is a heart experience. As we allow the Shepherd, the one who knows us and carries us close to his heart, to live in us, we can feel his loving arms. We grow stronger and more confident in this love. When we receive the gift of resurrection, believing that our souls live with God forever and that this world is not our home, we feel assurance. Out of this comfort, assurance, love, hope, and contentment, our souls are not just filled, but they can overflow. This won't happen until we receive, unwrap, and possess these precious gifts as our own. God is an amazing gift giver. Have you not only opened the gifts, but also touched them, put them on, reflected on them, tasted them, treasured them? When we allow ourselves to know that these gifts are really ours, our perspective changes. This shift has far-reaching effects. We now see life from a different dimension.

Gaining a New Perspective

Astronauts transition, not from one country to another, but from earth to outer space. When they return to earth, many report a paradigm shift in their thinking. According to Edgar Mitchell, Apollo 14 astronaut, "Something happens to you out there. You develop an instant global consciousness, a people orientation, an intense dissatisfaction with the state of the world, and a compulsion to do something about it."[34] Researchers of this phenomenon, like PsyD Jonah Paquette, have seen that such transformative experiences of awe bring greater feelings of connectedness to others and a realization that we are part of something much grander than ourselves. Their research shows that this often results in increased social connection, more kindness and generosity, and greater curiosity. Benefits include happiness, less materialism, more humility, and a greater desire to grow and change. Paquette recounts that Austrian psychologist Viktor Frankl describes a similar experience after his transition from imprisonment in a concentration camp during WWII to liberation.

> I walked through the country past meadows, for miles and miles, toward the market town near the camp. Larks rose to the sky and I could hear their joyous song. There was no one to be seen for miles around; there was nothing but the wide earth and sky and the larks' jubilation and the freedom of space. I stopped, looked around, and up to the sky—and then I went down on my knees. At that moment there was very little I knew of myself or of the world… How long I knelt there I can no longer recall. But I know that on that day, in that hour, my new life started. Step for step I progressed, until again I became a human being."[35]

---

34. Jonah Paquette, *Awestruck: How Embracing Wonder Can Make You Happier, Healthier, and More Connected* (Boulder, CO: Shambhala, 2020), 9–10.
35. Paquette, *Awestruck*, 19.

What Now, God?

These studies only confirm God's truths. When we see God, One so beyond our comprehendible dimension, it changes us. We can then realize that not only is God big and strong enough to sustain us through all kinds of changes, but he lovingly holds us close, leading us to the curl of the wave. When we are loved, we can return love. We love because he first loved us. When we find God, we realize we have something much greater than our circumstances to give. We are part of something much bigger than the transitions we are experiencing, no matter how overwhelming they seem. When we make that connection with God, we will realize that our transition is not just *our* transition; it is intricately related to a much bigger picture, one that God understands even when we do not.

The Ubuntu Principle, the African term for this interconnection, describes this metaphysical dynamic. As I write this chapter on the day we celebrate Martin Luther King Jr, I am reminded of his description of this reality through words taken from his 1965 commencement speech at Oberlin College:

> All life is interrelated, and we are all caught in an inescapable network of mutuality, tied in a single garment of destiny. Whatever affects one directly, affects all indirectly. For some strange reason I can never be what I ought to be until you are what you ought to be. And you can never be what I ought to be until I am what I ought to be—this is the interrelated structure of reality.

Not only has research supported the ways in which connection to something bigger than ourselves binds us together for a communal purpose, but it has also shown that it spurs those who see beyond their own situation to act more compassionately and generously toward others.

The Secret

The Apostle Paul thought he was on the way to Damascus. Little did he know the transitions coming his way. Life-altering, terribly hard but wonderfully fulfilling transitions would follow him throughout the remainder of his days. He learned the secret for navigating them:

> *I have learned to be content whatever the circumstances.*
> *I know what it is to be in need, and I know what it is to have plenty. I have learned the secret of being content in any and every situation, whether well fed or hungry, whether living in plenty or in want.*
> *I can do all this through him who gives me strength.* (Philippians 4:11b–13)

His secret for contentment was his connection with Jesus through the Spirit. Not knowledge of Jesus, but *connection* with him. Paul learned that he could not do anything on his own. This secret carried him through imprisonment, beatings, hardships, joys, victories, and finally through death. Remember, he also spent years in the desert before he proceeded with his God-given mission. Through all the changes, Paul kept going, knowing that he had an advocate, counselor, living water, bread, light, shepherd, and mentor. I close this chapter with Paul's prayer, "May the God of hope *fill* you with all joy and peace as you trust in him, so that you may *overflow* with hope by the power of the Holy Spirit" (Romans 15:13, emphasis added).

Then Sings My Soul
By Erika Walton Sitzberger
Chicagoland, Illinois

I know storms. Transition storms. Grief storms. Grey skies, cloudy thoughts, long pauses, and sadness still well up within me, causing internal floods from God knows where. I encounter the pain. I consciously examine it, floating into its ether. I find myself hemmed in by time and space, and the battle for my mind begins.

Sometimes it's like floating into a haze of despair, only to be pulled out by the constraint of time. Fortunately, though, everything in *this* world comes to an end. I am relieved that the twilight zone is not real. I am grateful that I make it through the storm of my mind. I rise above it, and peace comes in the nick of time.

I recently read about a young man, African American, twenty-one years of age and found dead lying in the street near his apartment, a few miles from the university he attended. Apparently, he was a brilliant student, a cellist, a budding composer, and a beautiful soul. The authorities still don't know what happened to him; they are looking for clues and for answers.

I ask myself, *Why do these horrific things happen? I ask the*

Lord, Why do you allow suffering and hidden sin? Why do human beings choose destruction over humanity? I still don't know. The storm can be brutal. Natural disasters, desertions, illnesses, violence, disregard for life, divorce, and abuse are among the disturbances that can overwhelm the human spirit.

So I pray, *Be with the ones who have lost a child, Lord, and the ones who are in jail. Be with the ones who risked their lives so others could be safe and so can no longer hold down a job. Lord, be with the mentally ill and the ones who need home healthcare. And be with the ones who have no country, no ID, and no health insurance. The young ones, the destitute and those who feel they have lost it all. And Lord God, please, be with me. Help me to fulfill your purpose today.*

In that delicate moment, my faith grows, and my soul begins to sing with God. Call it experience, call it wisdom, call it common sense, but I call him for help! Sometimes, when I look into the mirror after I have weathered a personal storm, I see God's image in me, even though I may still be sad. When I look into my eyes, I know my ancestors are rooting for me (Hebrews 12:1). They are electric and having a festive party. *Whew,* they say. *She is free and so are we!* They sing through my thoughts, my own personal chorus, *Little girl, you are sweet, little girl, it's complete, make art, make art, make art.*

Funny? I know it's strange, but here's the thing. I believe there is more to life than what we see. Even the wind is proof that there is something moving us along that our physical eyes cannot envision, although it is real! When I close my eyes, I can see color, I can see light. Beyond my line of vision and struggles, there is still beauty. And there is most certainly grace.

My precious mother, Estella Walton, loved to sing. She was a songbird. She passionately sang and lived out the song "Amazing

What Now, God?

Grace"[36] throughout her existence. We enjoyed our life traveling with The Crossroads Singers summer after summer, singing songs of redemption throughout my entire childhood. She is gone now, but knowing she walked through life singing with God helps me stand today. It helps me keep singing. I still find her pencil marks in the margins of her books and biblical commentaries. Her special, passionate notes reveal that she was strategizing her way to paradise. She was minding her progress, and tending to her soul. And you know what? I am, too.

Because I am still here, I will breathe. Because I am still here, I will take my time and sing my song. Because I am still here, I will live and share what I have learned with others. I am the Bluebird Singing Today (bluebirdsingingtoday.com).

---

36. https://www.youtube.com/watch?v=UnH6URCbws8&list=PLXsj2h2eNYAhSSpJW9axpfW2W_84gSDMv.

Reflections on Receiving and Overflowing

It can be difficult, at times, to read the Bible for purposes more than gathering information or measuring performance. God is the great giver and longs to fill us. It is only when we are filled that we can then give. Otherwise, we run on empty and burn out. Practice the exercise on receiving from the Word. Read the following verses as Jesus describes his life-giving gifts to us. Try reading them out loud, several times. Reading the Scriptures aloud, repetitively, often brings new insights. Read to receive as you read the following:

> Then Jesus declared, "I am the bread of life. Whoever comes to me will never go hungry, and whoever believes in me will never be thirsty." (John 6:35)

> When Jesus spoke again to the people, he said, "I am the light of the world. Whoever follows me will never walk in darkness, but will have the light of life." (John 8:12)

> "I am the good shepherd. The good shepherd lays down his life for the sheep...
>
> "I am the good shepherd; I know my sheep and my sheep know me—
> just as the Father knows me and I know the Father—and I lay down my life for the sheep."
> (John 10:11, 14–15)

What Now, God?

> *"I will not leave you as orphans; I will come to you.*
>
> *Before long, the world will not see me anymore, but you will see me. Because I live, you also will live. On that day you will realize that I am in my Father, and you are in me, and I am in you...*
>
> *But the Advocate, the Holy Spirit, whom the Father will send in my name, will teach you all things and will remind you of everything I have said to you.*
>
> *Peace I leave with you; my peace I give you. I do not give to you as the world gives. Do not let your hearts be troubled and do not be afraid."* (John 14:18–20, 26–27).

Make this a regular practice. Google a site that can help you practice a spiritual discipline like *Lectio Divina*, meant to help fill and refresh your soul.

Think about three "American proverbs." (These proverbs can also be proven scientifically.) Reflect on what these mean to you:

Contented cows give more milk.
Happy chickens lay more eggs.
You can't squeeze blood out of a turnip.

Chapter 7:
Courage for the Next Steps

I bring us back once again to the thought of riding the waves and finding their curls. It feels good to think of a Florida beach today, with the outside temperature in single digits where I am. Though I grew up in Florida, for nearly thirty-five years I have lived in New England. During these years, I may have set records for the amount of time it has taken me to get my body submerged in the cold New England waters. Just ask my kids. Since I often swim for exercise, I have finally made great progress in this area, but I much prefer a slow, steady transition where the temperature of the water allows for comfortable ease of access. But to get into the water, there is no shortcut for getting wet. Had I remained unmovable, I would have never entered the water in New England. Transitions require movement. Beginnings. Endings. New beginnings. None of these are simple.

While previous traumas may hinder our ability to "jump in" quickly, there are times we are forced to make transitions. We may wish to move forward but have a hard time making the jump. We prefer to stand and watch, thinking about how we wish we had the courage to go forward. I want to encourage you, if you are stuck from past traumas, to get some professional help. Being stuck from trauma is different from being hesitant to move forward. My son's childhood trauma as an orphan brought him obstacles that are different from mine but very real. People who have experienced various types of abuse often find themselves shutting down or reacting to changes quicker or more intensely than others without that background. My own "transition fears" stem more from fear of change, fear of disappointing someone, fear of inadequacy, or fear of regret.

I felt all these hesitancies this past year as I experienced dizzying transitions. I could not avoid the transition to widowhood, but I could have delayed retirement. I could have remained in my house. I could have stayed in my town and familiar surroundings, but something inside me felt the need for change. My house was bigger than I needed, and I also relived too many traumatic moments of trying to revive Wyndham during my last several years living there. I felt this urging inside, which I believe to be a calling.

Getting Wet

I thought and overthought about the transitions I was considering. I don't think my kids believed I would go through with the move, but once I decided to get in the water and transition on purpose, I repeatedly felt the curl of the wave. Of course, after I sold my house and officially pushed the retirement button, there were several moments of "What did I just do?!" And, for the first time, I was on my own. The decision had to be mine alone. Yes, I prayed fervently and sought counsel, but I had to be the one to jump into the water. I still live in New England, so, just like the icy water, the transitions took my breath away. I retired, I moved, and then I made my tuition payment, signaling the beginning of my doctorate journey, which, God willing, I will complete when I am seventy years old. Numerous times I have asked myself if I was crazy, but over and over, with each new decision and transition, God has affirmed my steps. I believe God often surprises us with tangible support when we jump into the water. Today, I told my daughter that I must officially qualify as a nerd, as I received my syllabus for my newest class and felt giddy with excitement after reading the assignments. I love where I live. I love what I am doing. I miss my husband fiercely. I love my new church. I love the new ways God is bringing me new opportunities to serve others. I miss my friends. Yet I would never have known this exuberance if I had only put my toe in the water and not felt the waves or found the curl.

Do You Still See the Rabbit?

I recently read a story of a wise man sitting on a farm in the sun with his dog. A person came to him for wisdom. As the person was sitting by the man and his dog, a rabbit ran by, and the man's dog took off. Soon other dogs began barking and chasing, but one by one they dropped off the pursuit. Only the man's dog continued the chase. The person seeking wisdom asked him why his dog was the only one to keep going. The man explained that only his dog had seen the rabbit. The other dogs had not seen the rabbit; they had only followed the commotion. He asked, "Are you chasing rabbits because you see commotion, or do you actually see the rabbit?"

It is all too easy to get involved in the commotion of transitions and forget what we are pursuing and why. Why have you chosen to do what you do? Are you just running with the commotion, or do you have a calling? In his outstanding book, *The Call,* Os Guinness shares, "People confront it [the call] in all the varying transitions of life—from moving homes to switching jobs to breakdowns in marriage to crises of health. Negotiating the changes feels longer and worse than the changes themselves because transition challenges our sense of personal meaning."[37]

What Are the Ancient Paths?

God calls each one of us. We secure a place in his narrative of love. Guinness continues, "To explore the truth of God's call is to appreciate what is nothing less than God's grand global project for the restoration and renewal of humanity and the earth—and our part in it."[38] Our call is more than any mission statement we might construct, any of the goals we seek, and any accomplishments we fulfill. Our call from God can feel like a winding road on a foggy day or at times a straight path on a clear day. Our calling is filled with wonder, uncertainty,

---

37. Os Guinness, *The Call: Finding and Fulfilling God's Purpose for Your Life* (Nashville, TN: Nelson, 2018), 3.
38. Guinness, *The Call,* xi.

and worship. The road we are currently traveling may feel far from our perceived call. So, how do we know we are heeding God's calling for us? We may not ever, this side of heaven, completely understand the twists and turns transitions bring to our paths or where they are leading us. Jeremiah advised well:

> *This is what the LORD says:*
>
> *"Stand at the crossroads and look;*
> *ask for the ancient paths,*
> *ask where the good way is, and walk in it,*
> *and you will find rest for your souls.*
> *But you said, 'We will not walk in it.'"*
> (Jeremiah 6:16)

So what were the ancient paths that Jeremiah referred to? They are the same paths that Abraham took when he was called to a place he didn't know, following God's lead day by day. These are the same ancient paths that by faith allowed him to trust God in seemingly impossible circumstances. They are the ancient paths that Moses traveled when he wandered in the wilderness for forty years, never reaching his goal of setting foot in the promised land, yet never letting go of God. This was the same ancient path that Naomi took when she was hopeless, depressed, and bitter—having nowhere to go but "home toward God." These are the paths Hagar took when she felt despair, yet found the God who sees and hears. These are the ancient paths. We may not know where the transitions are taking us, but his call for you and me can be summed up in two words from Jesus: "Follow me." When we do this, we will find rest for our souls, no matter the transition.

The Caller Behind the Call

Sometimes our call is clear. We feel God's Spirit moving to fulfill through us something God has gifted or prepared for us to do. It may involve a transition that scares us, such as moving to a mission field or selling stuff to become more generous to the poor. It may involve getting our hands dirty in an uncomfortable way. Sometimes, our life stage of raising young children in the nurture and admonition of the Lord is a very full calling. Callings change throughout our lives, but they never change from "Follow me." Today, I can follow God's calling in new ways that were not possible years ago, when my life situation was different due to family and local church responsibilities. Perhaps I was too busy to hear the same callings, or perhaps the time was not right.

Our sense of timing is not the same as God's, but as long as we have breath in us, God has a purpose for our lives. Transitions change our circumstances, but we can live with enthusiasm, gratitude, and joy when we assuredly follow God's call. I will use Guinness' words describing calling: "Calling is the truth that God calls us to himself so decisively that everything we are, everything we do, and everything we have is invested with a special devotion and dynamism lived out as a response to his summons and service."[39] Guinness continues with wisdom that applies to any transition we are experiencing or will experience:

> The secret of seeking [our calling] is not in our human ascent to God, but in God's descent to us. We start out searching, but we end up being discovered. We think we are looking for something; we realize we are found by Someone... What brings us home is not our discovery of the way home but the call of the Father who has been waiting there for us all along, whose presence there makes home home.[40]

To move forward through transitions, like the wise man's dog on chase, we must never lose sight of the rabbit. The most important thing about a calling is not the call, but the Caller.

The Community of Transition

Our Western cultural perspective thinks individually, but the culture of the Bible is communal. Our transitions not only affect us, but as we are part of God's family, they impact others as well. Our transitions affect our physical families. If we struggle to find our identity, we will seek certain expectations from our family members rather than give to them out of the fullness of our hearts. Then,

---

39. Guinness, *The Call*, 5.
40. Guinness, *The Call*, 15.

their reactions to our reactions tangle the web of unfulfilled longing. When we find God in our transitions, others' reactions become less important. Then we can, like Jesus, respond with love.

Also, we are not meant to carry our grief alone. Our families can be sharers or victims of our grief, depending on our acceptance of our identity and our vulnerability in mourning. Our calling affects more than us, and when it is purposed for the benefit of others, we more fully and quickly find rest for our souls. In a family, physical or spiritual, our transitions often collide, run parallel, or intersect with others' transitions. To avoid trainwrecks, we need some time to sort out the baggage accompanying our transitions and learn to hear how others are responding to our transition, dealing with transitions of their own, or both.

Often, our transitions set off transitions for others in our immediate circle. Take some time with your family or with close friends in the church to talk these through. Talk about ways the transitions affect you and them. Talk about the identity challenges the transitions bring. Be vulnerable in expressing grief. Pray with each other and offer hope. We all need hope. The phrase, "Be kind. Everyone is grieving," holds much truth.

We don't have to walk through transitions alone, and God does not intend that we do. His desire is that we all have a spiritual community. This is more than a "place to go" on Sunday. Community means we have people in our lives who know us because we let ourselves be known.

We let ourselves be vulnerable, and we speak life and truth from God to each other. We pray with and for each other. This spiritual community is a place where we can be honest and human together as we help each other think and act more like Jesus. Community is a place to be built up and to build up others. We need help and encouragement along the way, and we also need to be encouragers. As the Scriptures say, "It is more blessed to give than to receive" (Acts 20:35). Often, we find that offering a helping hand or listening ear brings unexpected peace, healing, and joy to our hearts. God works like that. Let us remember Jesus' "golden rule" as we help others through transitions: "Do to others as you would have them do to you" (Luke 6:31).

I have built some new and close relationships with others who are experiencing similar transitions. It is important to know we are not alone. As we change and if we look, we can find meaningful relationships to help us along the way.

> *Carry each other's burdens, and in this way you will fulfill the law of Christ.* (Galatians 6:2)

Find Your People
By Amber Effner
Woodstock, Georgia

About five years ago I moved jobs and houses, my kids changed schools, and my husband lost his job. For the next few years I placed a Band-Aid on my pain. I ate too much, watched too much television, and even drank in excess. Fast-forward to the pandemic. My daughter was graduating and not holding on to her faith. I was completely unaware of how far from God I had drifted.

While I was trying to teach classrooms of children from a computer screen, I fell into despair. Through a phone call with a trusted friend, God sent me a blessing: a circle of older women. We studied out grief and how to process it correctly. It turns out that I had been doing it wrong my whole life. I had unprocessed grief, still, from when I was a teenager!

I learned to journal. I learned how to run to God. I will never be perfect. I struggle; but now that circle provides a battleground to defeat my negative thoughts. All of us in the group are going through some sort of transition, but this is my story.

Through this journey, my entire family gave up alcohol and continues to get help with the negative dynamic with which we began our family. I cling to Paul's words, "Whatever is pure, whatever is lovely…" (Philippians 4:8). Sometimes I even feel guilty for the gratitude I have for the pandemic, because without it my circle, my precious, beautiful, grief circle, might not exist.

Loving People Through Transitions
By Pam George
Grand Rapids, Michigan

I have served in a leadership capacity for the past thirty years, and one of the hardest challenges I have faced as a leader is navigating transitions. I have been on both sides of personnel shifts. As a leader, I lacked knowledge and empathy to deliver the news of letting someone go. I have also been on the other side of that conversation. As I explored this topic as part of my doctoral research, I was pleasantly surprised to see how research aligned with the way Jesus handled transitions.

God has perfect ways of equipping us. A research assignment concerning transitions in the workplace prompted me to reflect on transitions in the ministry. Jesus, the master of transition, can help direct our journey to establish better transition practices.

At my workplace, I recall a situation in which a woman I respected had to step out of her leadership role. Soon after, she was plagued with depression, health challenges, and despair. She quit the organization. Nothing was said about it; there was just awkward avoidance. I decided to reach out to her. I was shocked to find this once confident, powerful woman I respected sitting, devastated, in her living room after years of serving in the organization. She had no emotional support or direction. Although she had received a severance package, there was no consideration for her psychological needs. I have witnessed the same devastation in the ministry. I have seen heroes I admired for their faith leave churches disillusioned, disunified, and desolate.

Certainly, there are examples of those who have adjusted well, but I am convinced we need more dialogue on how people experience transitions in varied ways so that we can meet people where they are and love them through the changes.

Major factors in organizational change include unspoken expectations and lack of communication. Studies by Barna Research show that transparent communication builds unity. Too often, they found, changes were viewed as surprising and abrupt, missing guidance and direction. Research by Ibarra and Scoular found that leaders often lack the relational and soft skills to ensure success. Those who were surveyed expressed grief caused by insensitivity, lack of warning, dialogue, failure to hear both sides, the involvement of a few decision makers, and lack of collective prayer and fasting involving all parties.

Best practice transitions included the provision of emotional support and relational nutrients, which include reaching out, listening, empathizing, helping the person find meaning in their transition, and recognizing that transitions bring grief. Speaking words such as, "You are not alone in this transition," produce endorphins that support them through the pain of change.[41] This advice echoes the Scriptures' teachings to love in action and truth. It follows Jesus' words recorded in Matthew 7:12, "So in everything, do to others what you would have them do to you, for this sums up the Law and the Prophets."

Surrounding Jesus' death, the disciples experienced despair, guilt, doubt, fear, threat, depression, and even suicide. Jesus' response shows us his priority in loving well. He met each of his disciples, who all responded to transition differently, in their emotional

---

41. John Townsend, People Fuel: *Fill Your Tank for Life, Love, and Leadership* (Grand Rapids, MI: Zondervan, 2019).

state and moved them forward. In John 20:15, Jesus responded to Mary by asking her why she was crying. He called her by name, validated her emotions, and validated her as a person. In John 20:19, when the disciples were locked in a room in fear, he showed up, offering them peace and direction. In 20:27, Jesus took time to clear Thomas' doubts. In John 21, the disillusioned disciples had gone back to fishing. Jesus displayed empathy, meeting them where they were, even encouraging them with a big catch and a hot breakfast. Jesus, in crucial transitional times, met the emotional needs of his disciples.

Transition is hard, and Jesus' example of empathy encourages me to engage with others who are in transition. I know I have needed this and will continue to need it. When we follow Jesus' example, we can more effectively love others through their transitions.

Reflections on Courage for the Next Steps

Reflect on what currently hinders you from finding the "curl of the wave" in your transitions. Fear? Past failures? Confusion? Shame? Loneliness?

Do you believe God still has a purpose for your life? If you cannot yet see it, is it enough to just be "his beloved?"

The chapter states, "To move forward through transitions, like the wise man's dog on chase, we must never lose sight of the rabbit... The most important thing about a calling is not the call, but the Caller." Do you identify more with the dogs caught up in the chase, or do you still "see the rabbit?" How can you better "see the rabbit?"

Do you think it is most important to understand your calling, or to believe that a relationship with the Caller is of utmost value? Reflect on your answer.

How do you practice community as you face transitions? Do you believe God means for us to live in community? If so, how might you make your spiritual community a more meaningful part of your life?

How do our transitions affect each other as we live together in our physical and spiritual families? Why is this important to consider?

What does it mean that God is always seeking to find you? How does this relate to your finding God in transitions?

Conclusion

The answer to the book title's question, "What Now?" can be summed up in the words of the subtitle, "Finding God." Since the beginning of humanity, God has been asking, "Where are you?" We find God when we realize he is looking for us. God always seeks us. When we begin to grasp the incredible love and sacrifice involved in his search for us, then we can find him. When we find him, we find ourselves, replacing our once misinformed, functional identity with a relational identity.

We are created in the image of God, loved by him, and made for relationship with him. We gain our meaning and purpose through him. Only him. Then, when change comes, we can still know who we are. We must learn to sit with grief, naming it in naked vulnerability with God while learning to lament. Though we may wish to run through the desert or skip it altogether, desert times can transform us, as they did for men and women who have gone before. It is often in the desert that we come to understand who God is, allowing us to accept who we are. In the desert, we can discover that he walks with us through our pain and also grieves with us. Expect the desert sometime, or several times throughout your Christian life journey.

As we enter this sacred space called transition, let us take time to form and recount our core convictions,

What Now, God?

making deeper God-connections that capture our hearts. As we connect with him, we create space to more readily accept and experience his powerful Spirit in our lives. This indescribable power carries us through all kinds of change.

As we remember God, let us then raise our ebenezers, to mark endings and beginnings—markers reminding us that God cares and goes with us. With this surety, we can gain courage to take steps forward. We may feel we are thrashing in the waves as transitions come crashing over our heads. We may feel we are treading water, never finding the shore. We may even feel we are drowning. Find that curl of the wave. For in that curl rests the loving, powerful, unstoppable Spirit of God. And with God, find your people. God intends for us to live in community. We need each other.

What now? Find God in your transitions. Don't fear asking help to find the curl. As I think back to my dad teaching me, I remember times when he picked me up to place me in just the right spot. He gave instruction, offered encouragement, and then let go and watched me ride. Once we find the curl, we want others to experience that sweet spot. As God's Spirit envelops every part of our being, he can carry us all the way to shore. We may arrive with sand-filled swimsuits and scraped legs, but oh, what a ride it is.

And now to him who can keep you on your feet, standing tall in his bright presence, fresh and celebrating—to our one God, our only Savior, through Jesus Christ, our Master, be glory, majesty, strength, and rule before all time, and now, and to the end of all time. Yes. (Jude 1:24–25 MSG)

Appendix: Who God Says We Are

A small sampling of scriptures concerning my identity as God's beloved:

I AM GOD'S...
- chosen (Ephesians 1:4; 1 Peter 2:9)
- image bearer (Genesis 1:27)
- child (John 1:12)
- possession (1 Corinthians 6:20)
- handiwork (Ephesians 2:10)
- friend (James 2:23-24)
- temple (1 Corinthians 6:19)
- coworker/partner (1 Corinthians 3:9)
- soldier (2 Timothy 2:3-4)
- ambassador (2 Corinthians 5:20)
- letter of recommendation (2 Corinthians 3:1-3)
- minister (2 Corinthians 3:6)
- beloved (Romans 1:7; 2 Thessalonians 2:13
- heir (Romans 8:17)
- apple of his eye (Psalm 17:8)
- delight (Zephaniah 3:17)

I HAVE BEEN...
- redeemed by his blood (1 Peter 1:18-19; Revelation 5:9)
- set free from sin and condemnation (Romans 8:1-2)
- set free from Satan's control (Colossians 1:13-14)

- set free from Satan's kingdom (Ephesians 2)
- chosen before the foundation of the world (Ephesians 1:4)
- predestined to be like Jesus (Romans 8:28-29)
- forgiven of all my sins (Colossians 2:13)
- washed in the blood of the Lamb (Revelation 1:5)
- given access to power, love, and self-discipline (2 Timothy 1:7)
- given the Holy Spirit (2 Corinthians 1:22)
- adopted into God's family (Romans 8:15)
- justified freely by his grace (Romans 3:24)
- given everything I need for a godly life (2 Peter 1:3)
- given great and precious promises (2 Peter 1:4)
- given God's seal of ownership (2 Corinthians 1:22)
- given the ministry of reconciliation (2 Corinthians 5:19)
- given authority over the power of the enemy (Romans 8:37-39; 1 John 4:4)
- given access to God (Ephesians 3:12)
- given wisdom (Ephesians 1:7-9)
- given the mind of Christ (1 Corinthians 2:16)
- heard (Psalm 40:1; 1 John 5:14)
- given a firm place to stand (Psalm 40:2)
- engraved on the palms of his hands (Isaiah 49:16)
- held by his hand (Psalm 73:23)
- guided with his counsel (Psalm 73:24)

I HAVE...

- access to the Father's grace (Romans 5:2)
- Christ in me (Colossians 1:27)

- a home in heaven waiting for me (John 14:1-2)
- all things in Christ (2 Corinthians 5:17–18)
- a living hope (1 Peter 1:3)
- an anchor to my soul (Hebrews 6:19)
- a hope that is firm and secure (Hebrews 6:19)
- the mind of Christ (1 Corinthians 2:16)
- confidence and access (Hebrews 10:19)
- peace with God (Romans 5:1)
- peace that passes human understanding (Philippians 4:7)
- divine access (2 Peter 1:4)
- protection in the shadow of his wings (Psalm 91:4)
- new life (Colossians 3:1; Romans 6:4)
- eternal life (Romans 6:23)
- confidence of my resurrection (John 11:25-26)
- purpose in life (2 Corinthians 5:4-5, 17-21)
- help and strength from God (Psalm 54:4)

Who I am in Christ: Biblical truths to "practice believing":

I AM...
- complete in him (Colossians 2:10)
- free from sin's power (Romans 6:14)
- sanctified (1 Corinthians 6:11)
- held by my right hand (Psalm 73:23)
- made fit for the Master's use (2 Timothy 2:21)
- loved eternally (1 Peter 1:5; Hebrews 13:5)
- eternally kept in the palm of his hand (John 10:29)

- kept from stumbling (Jude 1:24)
- kept by the power of God (1 Peter 1:5)
- not condemned (Romans 8:1-2)
- one with the Lord (1 Corinthians 6:17)
- a citizen of heaven, a member of God's household (Ephesians 2:19; Philippians 3:20)
- on my way to heaven (John 14:6)
- made alive by his mighty power (Ephesians 2:5)
- seated in heavenly places (Colossians 3:1-3; Ephesians 1:3)
- a candle in a dark place (Matthew 5:15)
- a city set on a hill (Matthew 5:14)
- the salt of the earth (Matthew 5:13)
- his sheep (John 10:14; Psalm 23; Psalm 100:3)
- hidden with Christ in God (Colossians 3:3; Psalm 32:7)
- protected from the evil one (1 John 5:18)
- shielded by God's power (1 Peter 1:5)
- secure in Christ (John 10:28-29)
- set on a Rock (Psalm 40:2)
- more than a conqueror (Romans 8:37)
- born again (1 Peter 1:23)
- a victor (1 John 5:4)
- healed by his wounds (Isaiah 53:56)
- covered by the blood of Jesus (Revelation 12:11; 1 Peter 1:19)
- sheltered under his wing (Psalm 91:4)
- hidden in the shadow of the Almighty (Psalm 91:1)
- sustained and helped (Psalm 54:4)

- carried close to his heart (Isaiah 40:11)
- presented to God without fault and with great joy (Jude 1:24)
- valued (Matthew 20:29-32)
- not alone (Matthew 28:20)
- filled with his love (Romans 5:5)

I CAN...
- do all things through Christ (Philippians 4:13)
- find mercy and grace to help (Hebrews 4:16)
- come with confidence to the throne of grace (Hebrews 4:16)
- extinguish all the flaming arrows (Ephesians 6:16)
- pray always and everywhere (Luke 21:36)
- defeat (triumph over) the enemy (Revelation 12:11)
- overcome temptation (1 Corinthians 10:13)
- find comfort in his compassion (2 Corinthians 1:3)

I CANNOT...
- be separated from God's love (Romans 8:35-39)
- be snatched from God's hand (John 10:28)
- be shaken (Psalms 16:8)
- be charged or accused (Romans 8:33)
- be condemned (1 Corinthians 11:32)

Acknowledgments

My heartfelt appreciation goes to the men and women who share their inspiring stories of finding God in transitions. Though their circumstances and ages vary, they all navigate their challenging transitions with honesty and faith. This book would not be the same without their valuable contributions. Thank you:

Hannah DeSouza

Angela Christoffel

Adam Birr

Judy McCreary

Chris Condon

Alexandra Ghoman

Erika Walton Sitzberger

Amber Effner

Pam George

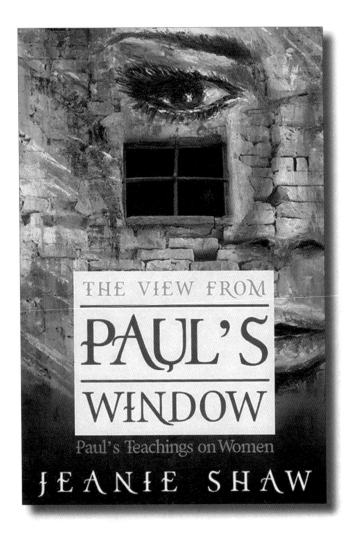

Available at www.ipibooks.com

Available at www.ipibooks.com

Available at www.ipibooks.com

Available at www.ipibooks.com

www.ipibooks.com